REVISED AND UPDATED

MINI-LATHE
TOOLS & PROJECTS

FOR HOME MACHINISTS

DAVID FENNER

Revised and updated by **George Bulliss**,
editor of *The Home Shop Machinist* magazine

FOX CHAPEL
PUBLISHING

Parts of this book were updated for today's American reader with regard to new techniques and tools. These updates were graciously provided by George Bulliss of *The Home Shop Machinist*, *Machinist's Workshop*, and *Digital Machinist* magazines.

First published in the United Kingdom by Special Interest Model Books
© Special Interest Model Books Ltd 2012
First published in North America in 2018 by Fox Chapel Publishing, 903 Square Street, Mount Joy, PA 17552.

ISBN 978-1-56523-916-6

Library of Congress Cataloging-in-Publication Data

Names: Fenner, David, 1944- author.
Title: Mini-lathe tools & projects for home machinists / David Fenner.
Other titles: Mini-lathe tools and projects for home machinists
Description: Mount Joy : Fox Chapel Publishing, 2018. | Includes index.
Identifiers: LCCN 2017034288 | ISBN 9781565239166 (pbk.)
Subjects: LCSH: Turning (Lathe work) | Lathes.
Classification: LCC TT207 .F466 2018 | DDC 684/.08342--dc23
LC record available at https://lccn.loc.gov/2017034288

To learn more about the other great books from Fox Chapel Publishing, or to find a retailer near you, call toll-free 800-457-9112 or visit us at *www.FoxChapelPublishing.com*.

We are always looking for talented authors. To submit an idea, please send a brief inquiry to acquisitions@foxchapelpublishing.com.

Printed in Singapore
First printing

CONTENTS

PREFACE

This book follows on from and refers to *Mini-Lathe for Home Machinists* (978-1-56523-695-0), and presents a selection of projects which are intended to extend the versatility of this little machine. In some cases, additional machining capacity will be required, which you may find at your local model engineering club.

While aimed at the Mini-Lathe, some projects can equally be applied to other small model engineering lathes and, in many cases, concepts can be scaled to suit other equipment.

Throughout this book, mention is made of *Model Engineers' Workshop* magazine (*MEW*), which is published in the UK by My Hobby Store Ltd (*www.myhobbystore.com*).

CHAPTER 1
THE MARK 2 MINI-LATHE

Since the publication in 2008 of the original edition of my book, *Mini-Lathe for Home Machinists,* the world has moved on.

The lathe used as the subject for that book was supplied by Arc Euro Trade, and was manufactured in China by Sieg. Never a firm to rest on its laurels, Sieg has raised its game with a revised version of this popular little machine **(Photo 1.01)**. Probably the most significant change, although not the most obvious one, is the motor, where the D.C. brushed motor has now been replaced with a brushless type. This type of motor has become very popular in aero-modeling circles, where the advantage of high power in a small package is particularly important.

As with the earlier model, this is a machine which is sold either "Factory Assembled" or "Arc Prepared." This essentially means that, while these machines will function adequately "out of the box," the performance can be substantially improved by careful strip down and rebuild/readjustment. I gave details of the suggested work in my *Mini-Lathe* book.

The data plates on the old and new machines give a flavor of the changes. The motor power has escalated from 350 watts

1.01 *New Mini-Lathe. The main visible changes are the control panel and leadscrew guard*

1.02 *My Heath Robinson torque measurement by wooden clamp brake and hanging scale*

1.03 *Depth of cut here is 2.3mm*

to 500 watts (it's now about 2/3hp), and the between-centers dimension has increased by 50mm to 400mm.

Sieg lathes are sold by a variety of vendors, some with the same dimensions and motors mentioned and some with slight modifications. All, however, share a similar construction.

HEADSTOCK

Apart from the leadscrew guard, the noticeable changes are all in this area. Because the motor is controllable from high (about 2500 rpm) down to very low (about 50 rpm) speed, the high/low speed gear change is no longer necessary. I first thought that this might compromise the machine's ability to remove metal, particularly at low rpm. As a means of investigating this, I rigged up the torque-measuring arrangement, which can be seen in **Photo 1.02**. On the original Mini-Lathe, running at about 250 rpm in low gear, I could wind up the adjuster nut until the overload tripped with the scale showing about 3 Kg. The revs had dropped by about 40 rpm just prior to tripping.

On the new machine at the same speed, it had not tripped at over 4 Kg, and at this stage the torque brake was getting seriously

1.04 *On the new machine, the belt drive is directly from motor to spindle...*

hot. Interestingly, the revs did not seem to drop although the motor sound did change, suggesting that the system was working hard. In general, the new machine runs more smoothly and quietly, probably because it no longer uses gears in the power transmission to the spindle. **Photo 1.03** shows a rudimentary test using a piece of 22mm mild steel. After I

1.06 *Shows the new chuck guard hinge and safety switch. Also visible is the tacho speed read out*

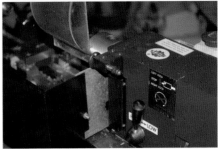

1.05 *...while on the old, the drive is taken to a counter shaft with two-speed gear selection*

1.07 *Older-style chuck guard hinge and safety switch*

adjusted the topslide, it was possible to take a cut of 0.090in. (2.33 mm) without chatter.

Compare **Photo 1.04** of the new change gear train with **Photo 1.05** of the old one. Slight changes have been made to the light alloy casting, and also to the gear cover, and the drive is now direct from the motor to the spindle, since the two-speed counter shaft is no longer present.

One small change concerns the chuck guard safety switch: compare new **Photo 1.06** with old **Photo 1.07**.

Regarding the electrical controls, the old machine had a built-in tachometer readout. On the new version, this feature is an optional extra, which plugs in and can be attached by magnets to the top of the headstock **(Photo 1.08)**. Motor speed is controlled by a rotary knob, marked between zero and 2500 rpm,

1.08 *View of new style control panel with add-on speed read out*

1.09 *Full-length guard to keep swarf, fingers and loose clothing from contacting leadscrew*

and it is likely that this will allow sufficiently accurate speed selection for most purposes. Those wishing for higher precision in speed control can simply plug in the readout.

Having fitted the tachometer set, it was possible to set the knob against the line graduations and compare with actual revs. The following readings were noted:

Knob setting	Tacho readout
100	0
200	90
300	270
400	410
500	580
1000	1020
1500	1560
2000	2080
2500	2490

One visible change is the inclusion of a guard for the leadscrew **(Photo 1.09)**. Apparently this is now a Health and Safety requirement for some markets. On the plus side, the guarding certainly keeps swarf from becoming lodged in the leadscrew thread, while on the minus, it causes a change from a two to one clasp half nut.

I have not been able to confirm this point, but it looks possible to modify the new machine to its "old" status by removing the guard and adding the second half nut. Assuming this to be correct for owners who prefer the old two half nut arrangement, it is likely that the spare parts to retrofit will in due course be on offer.

SUMMARY

The new Mini-Lathe has now acquired some serious power. For the older machine, the makers claimed a lowest speed of 100 rpm. For the newer model, the practical bottom of the range is probably about 60 to 70 rpm. If you look at one of these little machines, remember it now has a 2/3hp motor (many Myfords have 1/2hp) so do not be tempted to try holding the chuck to stall the motor. It now has real bite.

CHAPTER 2
IMPROVING THE RADIUS TURNING ATTACHMENT

In the final chapter of my *Mini-Lathe* book, I commented briefly on this device, and at the time introduced two easy upgrade modifications, these being 1) add shims to bring the pivot centers up to lathe centerline height, and 2) add a wavy washer to avoid endfloat of the frame on its bearings. The first of these ensured that spheres, rather than lemon-shaped parts, could be produced; the second would make it easier to keep the tool point on centerline. At the time, I also noted that it would be advantageous to improve the location arrangements for the toolbit, and to add some form of controlled radial infeed. These two points have now been addressed.

On the device as supplied, the cutting tool is clamped in a milled oval slot by two Allen screws. Due to the oval shape, it has several millimeters of sideways latitude. By inserting a short length of steel backing having a semicircular section, and by clamping the tool against it, the bit now benefits from having a fixed location in two planes. This secondary clamping needs only to be a "nip up," and is achieved by means of an added M6 Allen screw, applying thrust via a short piece of drill rod.

To add screw adjustment of the radial setting, remove the existing handle and add two standoffs which carry a bridge piece.

2.01 *Modified swing frame assembly*

This, in turn, houses an M6 adjuster screw and a new handle made slightly longer than the original. **Photo 2.01** shows the modified swing frame assembly.

NEW PARTS

Before moving forward and cutting metal, I strongly suggest that prospective upgraders start by measuring the swing frame casting. The sizes given for the various components derive from those given for the swing frame casting in **Fig 2.1.** Bearing in mind that the general dimensions are not machined, some variation may be encountered and, if so, alter the design as necessary.

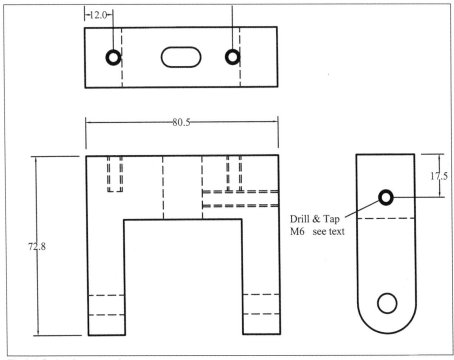

Fig 2.1 *Swing frame casting*

BACKING

As can be seen in **Photo 2.02,** I placed a length of 8mm diameter steel bar in the vise on the mill table with sufficient protruding to make the part. I progressively milled down this overhanging section until it reached half of the original thickness. I then cut off this

2.02 *Milling the backing piece*

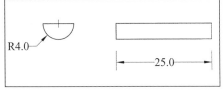

Fig 2.2 *Half round backing*

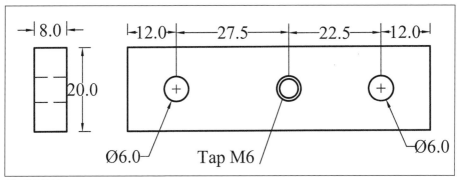

Fig 2.3 *Bridge*

piece, the ends being tidied up by file to match the thickness of the cast frame. The detail is given in **Fig 2.2**.

BRIDGE

An overlength piece of 20mm x 8mm steel flat was set up in the mill, and the three holes spotted (**Photo 2.03**). These were then drilled or tapped as **Fig 2.3**. It was then finished to length.

2.03 *Spotting the hole positions on the bridge*

STANDOFF (FIG 2.4)

I then cut two lengths of 8mm across the flats (AF) steel hex, then faced to length. I used 8mm AF, as some was in stock. Feel free to increase to 10 or perhaps even 12mm AF. Round bar would also be perfectly acceptable, although a feature would then be needed for tightening, e.g. a cross-drilled hole or couple of flats. The required lengths were turned down to 6mm dia. (**Photo 2.04**) and the M6 threads added using a tailstock-guided die holder (**Photo 2.05**). It is worth pointing out here that typical dies cut differently on their front (usually carrying the size data) and rear faces. The front will usually have a significant taper entry (a sort of inverse situation to a tap), whereas the rear will have less. The effect of this can be seen in **Photo 2.06**, which shows one standoff

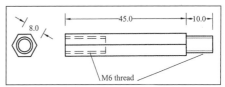

Fig 2.4 *Standoff*

2.04 *Turning down the standoffs ready for threading*

2.05 *Threading using a tailstock guided dieholder*

2.06 *Upper component threaded using die normally; lower has second operation with die reversed, taking thread closer to shoulder*

2.07 *Drilling hole for second standoff*

threaded using the die normally (front face leads) while the other has undergone a second operation using the die reversed. This technique can help get the thread a little nearer a shoulder. I then reversed the parts in the chuck, drilled and tapped M6.

ADJUSTER (FIG 2.5)

For simplicity, I constructed this from two parts, one length of M6 threaded rod, and a piece of 25mm diameter free-cutting mild steel to make the knob, which is a straightforward turning and tapping exercise. As the photos show, at this stage, I have not taken time to add the divisions. The pitch of the screw is 1mm, or 0.03937in., so one might choose to go for 40 divisions (each approximating to 0.001in.) or 50 (each being exactly 0.02mm).

To assemble, the rod is screwed into the knob and retained with Loctite. However, before doing this, it is worth finishing the other end in the lathe to avoid any "swash" effect, which could introduce adjustment errors.

HANDLE AND PUSH ROD

The push rod is simply cut from ³⁄₁₆in. dia drill rod, the ends being tidied up in the lathe. I cut the handle from ½in. diameter aluminum, drilled and tapped at one end, then added a little aesthetic embellishment for fun. I then Loctited in a short piece of the ubiquitous M6 steel threaded rod, to give a higher strength male thread.

MODIFICATION TO CASTING

Two additional tapped holes are needed, one to take the second standoff **(Photo 2.07)**, the other to accommodate the push rod and secondary clamp screw **(Photo 2.08)**. Positions for these are shown in **(Fig 2.1)**.

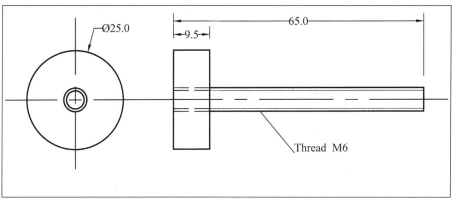

Fig 2.5 *Adjuster*

2.08 *Hole to take secondary clamp screw and push rod*

2.09 *Sub-assembly left to cure*

ASSEMBLY

I coated the half round surface of the backing with a smear of Loctite, and slipped it into position. I then inserted the HSS tool, and partially tightened the two original clamping screws. I then inserted the push rod and also partially tightened the new clamp screw. I then fully tightened the original two and left the Loctite to cure **(Photo 2.09)**.

I fitted each of the two standoffs, using a washer to accommodate the thread runout which remained. The bridge was located and held by one new Allen screw and the handle. Finally, I added the adjuster screw.

A BRIEF ASIDE ON FITTING THREADED PARTS TO TAPPED HOLES

I pointed out earlier that a second operation with a reversed die would bring the thread closer to a shoulder, but, nevertheless, washers were introduced under the standoffs. It may be worth briefly reviewing the general situation and the various design options available.

Clearly, if the male thread has a significant runout toward a shoulder, and if we try to screw this into a typical tapped hole, then it will bind as the thread starts to run out, and this will be before the shoulder makes face contact.

Three options may be considered, either in isolation or in combination.

The undercut may be turned on the male part, reducing the size close to the shoulder to the minor thread diameter, and extending out for a length, which removes the runout.

The threaded hole in the female part may be drilled out to the major thread diameter for a length which will accommodate the male thread runout.

A washer or spacer may be introduced, having the same effect, so that only fully formed threads are engaged.

CHAPTER 3

TAILSTOCK "OFF CENTER" FOR TAPER TURNING

In Chapter 5, I will describe a taper turning attachment, capable of dealing with a wide range of tapers. However, note that one of the accepted setups for taper turning involves working between centers and moving the tailstock center away from the lathe centerline. If the tailstock itself is moved in this manner, then there follows the inconvenience of setting it accurately back to datum for normal working. Devices have been proposed in the past to avoid this hassle (e.g. that by Peter Rawlinson in *Model Engineers' Workshop* Issue 108). However, I hope that the design offered here will be easily constructed by the relative novice with basic equipment.

It has been sized to suit the Mini-Lathe, with minimal projection toward the operator. I anticipate that the concept can easily be adapted for other machines. Off center devices which I have seen in the past have utilized the Morse taper feature of the tailstock for location, with the attendant possibility of rotational slippage. Location here is therefore by means of a clamp, acting on the outside diameter of the tailstock barrel.

No great precision is needed in making the parts; the only feature which should be precisely positioned is the hole for the center. As this is machined on the lathe, accurate

3.01 *Front view of "Off center"*

3.02 *Rear view of gadget*

height is automatically achieved. Front and rear views of the assembled article, off the machine, are shown in **Photos 3.01** and **3.02**.

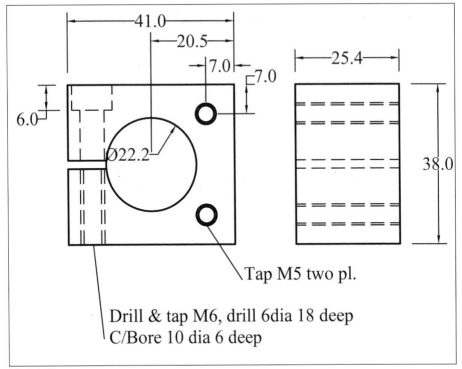

Fig 3.1 *Clamp*

Figure dimensions and notes:
41.0
20.5
7.0
7.0
25.4
6.0
Ø22.2
38.0

Tap M5 two pl.

Drill & tap M6, drill 6dia 18 deep
C/Bore 10 dia 6 deep

3.03 *Drilling holes in advance of tapping*

MAKING THE PARTS CLAMP (FIG 3.1)

Before starting on this, I carefully measured the tailstock barrel with a micrometer, and a test gage turned up to precisely this diameter from a piece of steel bar.

I then cut a piece of aluminum flat for the clamp, approximately to length then squared up by turning the faces, the work being held in the four jaw chuck. It was then marked out for the position of the bore, and located again in the four jaw, to machine this feature, by first drilling, then finally boring to size so that the test gage would enter smoothly over the full depth.

I then drilled **(Photo 3.03)** the two M5 holes and tapped. I carved the slot by using a ¹⁄₁₆in. slitting saw in the mill. Alternatively, it might

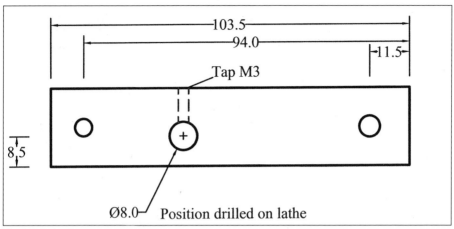

Fig 3.2 *Swing bar*

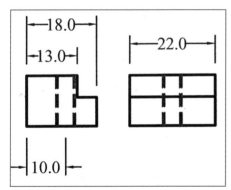

Fig 3.2A *Swing clamp*

3.04 *Milling step*

be simply cut with a hacksaw. A little further work on the clamp will be required later. It is necessary to file a slot to clear the swing clamp, as it moves around in an arc. The slot is just visible in **Photo 3.02.**

SWING BAR AND CLAMP (FIG 3.2 & 3.2A)

The material for each of these is ⅞in. x ½in. mild steel flat. For the bar, I sawed off a length of 103.5mm and tidied the ends with a file. I then drilled the two bolt holes, one 5mm dia, the other 6mm. Note that the 8mm dia location for the center is dealt with later. Moving on to the clamp, here, the step was milled out first **(Photo 3.04)** and the hole drilled and tapped M5, then sawed off the appropriate length off the bar.

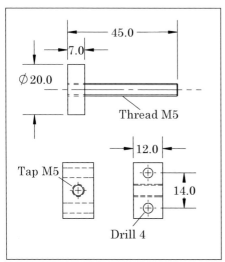

Fig 3.3 *Adjuster block and screw*

3.05 *Center location is positioned on lathe*

3.06 *Drilling position for locking screw*

ADJUSTER BLOCK AND SCREW (FIG 3.3)

The block is another cutting from the ⅞in. x ½in. bar, in which two holes are drilled 4mm diameter, and one drilled and tapped M5. The screw is drawn as a single turned part, but for simplicity was made by Loctiting a knurled aluminum head to a piece of M5 threaded rod, following the example given earlier for the radius turning attachment.

BACKPLATE (FIG 3.4)

The preferred material here would be bright mild steel plate. However, as I had none available, I utilized a piece of black plate, taking off the mill scale on the linisher. Drill and tap M6 the pivot position for the swing bar, then transfer the hole centers from the clamp, then drill and countersink these two features.

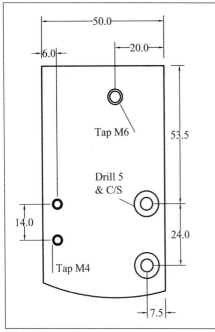

Fig 3.4 *Backplate*

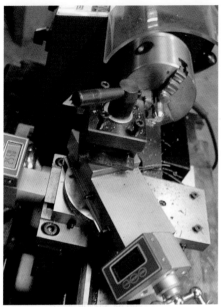

3.07 *Setup for turning 60-degree point*

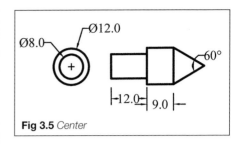

Fig 3.5 *Center*

Similarly mark or spot the adjuster block screw holes and drill/tap M4.

Now assemble the various parts, with the adjuster screw wound well back and the swing bar biased back against it. Clamp the assembly to the tailstock barrel and fit a center drill to the lathe chuck. Now use the center drill to start the location hole for the center **(Photo 3.05)**. Remove the bar, drill out and ream to 8mm. Drill the bar and tap M3 into the 8mm bore **(Photo 3.06)** to accommodate a locking screw for the center.

3.08 *Device fitted to lathe*

CENTER

Fig 3.5 depicts a typical 60-degree center. The one shown in the photos was made from mild steel, the setup for turning the point being illustrated in **Photo 3.07**. A more durable item might be machined from drill rod (then hardened) or perhaps by setting in a carbide point. Note that, as the tailstock center is moved progressively further out of alignment with the headstock, the engagement of the conical centers becomes less than ideal. To counter this, Peter Rawlinson advocated spherical centers, which would, of course, engage correctly for a wide range of work angles. Other variations might include a female center.

AESTHETICS

In this chapter, I have endeavored to present a gadget which is both easy and quick to make. The general appearance might be improved by sawing away some of the surplus material on the backplate, and spending a little more time cleaning up those surfaces which have suffered long storage and slight rusting.

CONCLUSION

Purists will correctly point out that, because the center is moved in an arc, it may also move away from the correct center height. By shifting the angular position of the clamp on the tailstock barrel, this tendency can be eliminated. Should a slight height error remain, the article by Peter McQueen (*Model Engineers' Workshop* Issue 81) demonstrated that there will be little effect on the accuracy unless the component geometry combines a large taper angle with small diameter.

Another author (Don Unwin in *Model Engineers' Workshop* Issue 99) voiced the view that an attachment must be quick and easy to fit and remove, or it will not get used. I like to add the rider that, unless it is quick and easy to make, it will not get made. I hope this one qualifies on both counts. **Photo 3.08** shows the accessory in place on the Mini-Lathe.

CHAPTER 4

MINI-LATHE SADDLE ADJUSTMENT

Given the low price of the various incarnations of the Mini-Lathe, it is no wonder that some aspects of the design owe more to accountancy than engineering. The means by which the saddle slideway adjustment is performed is a notable instance, and I was prompted to revisit this after adding the long cross slide which is described in Chapter 9. The added weight and leverage exposed the shortcoming of my earlier setting of this adjustment.

For the benefit of readers who may not have read my earlier *Mini-Lathe* book, the adjustment in the vertical plane is effected by cast strips fitted with opposing "pull me – push you" screws. By contrast, in the case of my *circa* 1960 Myford S7, clearance is set by bolting up hard against laminated shims.

IMPROVEMENT STRATEGIES

At the outset I aimed to consider four approaches. The first would require nothing more than careful measurement and a little work with a file. The second would be a sort of miniaturized version of the arrangement commonly used on lathe raising blocks. Number three would draw on the proven shim arrangement, and the fourth could employ taper gib strips.

Much useful information may be found on the *www.mini-lathe.com* website with links to work by Vikki Ford and Rick Kruger, including their versions of taper gib strips. Modifications for the first three strategies are very straightforward, and no specific advice should be needed. However, some comments and sketches are given relating to the taper gib arrangement.

DISMANTLING AND MEASURING

Ensure that the leadscrew clasp nuts are disengaged, then remove the two cap head screws **(Photo 4.01)** which retain the apron. This can then be slid along out of the way toward the tailstock. At this stage, clean any residual grease from the parts.

Then using a 0 to 1 in. or 25mm micrometer, take two measurements at each of four locations. **Photo 4.02** shows the micrometer

4.01 *Remove the two cap head screws to detach the apron*

4.02 *Micrometer positioned to measure thickness of saddle*

4.03 *Measure top of saddle to underside of bed*

positioned to check the thickness of the saddle, while **Photo 4.03** shows it placed to measure the height from top of saddle to underside of the bed. This is repeated at both sides of the cross slide for the front and then for the rear of the bed. The difference in each case I found to be 0.029in. This dimension then gives a benchmark for setting.

STRATEGY ONE

As supplied, the two pusher screws have typical ends, i.e. not perfectly square, and hence it could be easier for the plate to rock on the screws. The ends of the screws were filed flat by the simple method of screwing then out to protrude slightly, nipping up the locknut, then gently filing back flush with the surface **(Photo 4.04)**.

Using a thirty thousandths pack of feeler gages and a surface plate, the screws were then wound out to protrude by just that amount, then locked. I then trial re-fitted the strips to the lathe and, as can be seen in **Photo 4.05**, hex head screws were substituted for the original cap heads, as the leadscrew gets in the way of an Allen key and impedes adjustment.

4.04 *Screws are filed back flat and flush with surface*

4.05 *Reassembled with hex head bolts*

As the retaining screws are tightened, there is a theoretical one thousandth gap but, with just a gentle tweak, the strip will be deflected to reduce this. If the carriage movement is found to be smooth, then dismantle, apply grease, and reassemble. If not, check measurements and reset.

The flatted screw ends should offer improved stability for the strips, and given the time taken, this is a very quick and easy first move. However, we still have an arrangement by which the clamping screws must not be over-tightened, as doing so may bend or possibly fracture the strips.

4.06 *Tapping new strip*

While I believe that this quick fix did give an improvement, notable drawbacks remain. As the screws are not tightened hard up, it is still therefore possible for them to work loose in service. Additionally, as the screws are tightened, the strips become slightly bent, so that contact with the underside of the bed will occur in three areas rather than the along the whole length.

STRATEGY TWO

The deflection problem noted in Strategy One occurs because the screw forces are applied at different locations along the strip, causing bending. Strategy Two aims to bring the forces to common points, allowing the strip to remain straight and keep the whole of the mating surfaces in engagement.

New strips were cut from 20mm x 8mm steel flat, then drilled and tapped ⅜in. x 32 tpi in two positions **(Photo 4.06)** corresponding to the outer two clamping screws. A test nut was also made at this stage.

Two hollow jacking screws were then turned and screwcut to give a tightish fit in the test nut. These screws were then fitted and the strip assembled to the machine. Again, hex head bolts were substituted for the

4.07 *Adjustment is easier using two open ended wrenches*

original cap screws, and using two open end wrenches, it was a straightforward exercise to obtain a good running fit **(Photo 4.07)**.

The fit of the hollow screws in the tapped threads is important. If loose, then the strip would be able to cant slightly away from the horizontal, upsetting the adjustment. A way to get over this would be to add slots and small (perhaps 6BA or M2) clamp screws to ensure that the thread is gripped firmly and the strip held in its correct angular orientation. Note that, if using 8mm thick material, then when fitted to the position at the front of the saddle, a little material must be removed to clear the gear shaft and gear.

STRATEGY THREE

Given the proven success of the arrangement, I chose to look at the shimming option. Whereas the Mini-Lathe employs three clamp and two jack screws for each strip, the corresponding Myford assembly uses just two screws pulling hard up on the laminated shim packs. Strategy Three therefore follows this principle. I cut a number of shims and punched holes using the Roper Witney device **(Photo 4.08)**. To follow this through properly, one really needs a selection of shims allowing thickness packs to be made up in increments of about 0.001in.

Such a pack might be composed of shim metal of various thicknesses (aluminium Coke cans will give about 0.003in.) together with the proverbial cigarette paper. The difficulty I encountered was that of keeping all the bits together, although this might have been achieved with a dab of grease.

Correctly set, and using two screws per strip, this arrangement would allow them to be tightened up hard. For any reader keen to pursue the shim pack strategy, it may be worth noting that laminated shims are available as spares from Myford Ltd.

4.08 *Shims cut using punch*

STRATEGY FOUR

The respected Frank Hoose website, *www.mini-lathe.com*, gives a wealth of information on these popular machines, and in turn links to other sites. Vikki Ford's site covers a variety of topics including aluminum casting, but more relevantly, a taper gib arrangement for the Mini-Lathe saddle. On the site, it is noted that some difficulty was experienced machining the tapered parts, and the solution adopted was to glue the mating items together then machine as a parallel assembly.

A taper arrangement gives the advantage of easy and very fine adjustment to compensate for wear. I chose to use a taper of 1 in 40, controlled by an M4 adjustment screw. This would mean that one full turn of the screw would alter the saddle adjustment by approximately six-tenths of a thousandth. This fine level of control allows the machine to be set with "real feel."

Two points need to be noted. Unless the arrangement is shortened, it will project beyond the saddle. In the rear location, built to the hand shown, this meant that my rear saddle clamp would have to be removed or repositioned on the chuck side of the saddle. Also, if applying the design to the front shear, then material must be cut away to clear the shaft and gear which engages with the rack.

MANUFACTURE

One of the dangers of designing and making "on the hoof" is the potential for getting things wrong, and that is precisely what happened here. For some reason, I had adopted the erroneous mental fixation that the gib surface would be about thirty thousandths higher than the underside of the saddle, whereas it is actually about that amount lower. As a result, the taper was cut with this in mind, giving a height error

4.09 *Bracket part machined and roughly marked out*

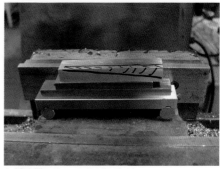

4.10 *Mill setup uses sine bar*

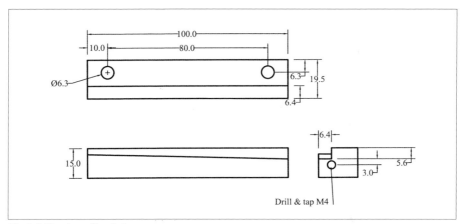

Fig 4.1 *Aluminum Bracket*

of about sixty thousandths. This could have been corrected either by remachining the bracket or by introducing spacers. I chose the latter, and the drawings reflect this because I believe this approach can lead to easier workholding when cutting the taper gib.

The first part to be made was the bracket **(Fig 4.1)**. In my case this started life as a length of aluminum extrusion which I milled down to give a rectangular section of 19.5mm x 15mm x 100mm long. Other sizes will work, such as ¾in. x ½in. – just adjust the dimensions to suit. **Photo 4.09** shows the

work at this stage, with rough markings of the position for the taper slot.

To cut the taper, I located a five inch sine bar in the milling vise, one end being jacked up with a small piece of ⅛in. plate. This would give the incline of 1 in 40 mentioned earlier. The tapered recess could then be carved out **(Photo 4.10)** taking the maximum depth to 0.220in., or 5.6mm. The M4 location for the adjuster screw was later drilled and tapped.

It is, of course, possible to eliminate the spacers by increasing the maximum cutting depth to 7.1mm. However this may raise workholding implications, or require a small amount to be shaved off the bracket when machining the gib.

To cut the taper gib **(Fig 4.2)**, I employed the bracket as a fixture to present the length of ¼in. square aluminum at the angle, allowing horizontal cuts to be taken from the top surface. The height of the assembly was set carefully in the vise by adding thin packing strips to a parallel **(Photo 4.11)**. As the cutter stays some 30 thousandths above the bracket, giving extra clamping room, I believe there may be an advantage in this approach, rather than cutting down a further 60 thousandths.

To clamp the gib in place, I cut a strip of card used as sacrificial packing to ensure that the vise jaw applied pressure via the gib and not just to the bracket **(photo 4.12)**. At this stage, the gib material was left overlength.

After assembly with the spacer(s) noted below, I marked a position for the slot which would engage with the adjuster screw. I then milled this transversely using a ³⁄₃₂in. diameter cutter.

To give the necessary spacing, I cut two pieces of ¹⁄₁₆in. thick gage plate, each with a 6.35mm hole. An improved approach could be to make one part 100m long with two holes spaced at 80mm. The adjuster screw **(Fig 4.3)** was a straightforward turning job using free-cutting mild steel (12L14).

The thread was first created using a die, after which the work was reversed, held in a collet to reduce gripping damage to the thread, and the head turned. (Purists might wish to make a threaded holder.) Aim for a snug fit between the flange and the slot already cut in the gib.

Finally, I cut a screwdriver slot by the simple means of a hacksaw. The completed assembly can be seen fitted to the lathe in **Photo 4.13.**

Fig 4.2 *Taper gib strip*

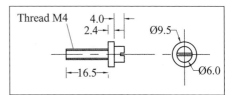

Fig 4.3 *Adjuster screw*

4.11 *Height set using thin material*

4.12 *Sliver of card added to gib thickness*

4.13 *Taper gib assembly fitted to lathe*

OPERATIONAL EXPERIENCE

The simple mod given as S1 is quick to achieve but still needs a degree of care in setting up. S2 still needed care and a sensitive touch, but I found it easier to manipulate a pair of open ended wrenches rather than two Allen keys or one Allen key and one wrench for S1. In theory, the shim technique, S3, should give a good result, but in practice I found it tricky to set up. No doubt working with "proper" laminated shims would be an improvement.

The taper gib really was a revelation. As noted before, a full turn of the screw gives vertical movement of just over half a thousandth. So rotating the screw by, say, one-tenth of a turn will close the gap by about a twentieth of a thousandth. There really is no skill or careful "feel" needed here; just turn the screw and check how the saddle slides. It was very quick and easy to obtain a very smooth running setup.

CHAPTER 5
TAPER TURNING ATTACHMENT

There are several accepted methods of turning tapers on a lathe. The most convenient is usually to swing the topslide around to the required half angle, lock the saddle position, and feed longitudinally by means of the topslide. There are typically two limitations here. Firstly, the length of taper is restricted by the topslide travel, and secondly, the angular graduations will not permit a high degree of accuracy in setting the angle. It is, of course, possible to set the angle accurately, using other equipment such as a sine bar.

The next method is to offset the tailstock center. The work is then mounted between centers and assumes an axis at the chosen angle to the lathe. This can work well for small angle tapers, but introduces the inconvenience of having to reset to datum after the job is completed. A variation on this theme is to add an accessory having an adjustable tailstock center, which incorporates variable offset, such as that described in Chapter 3.

Finally, we have the traditional taper turning attachment, typified by the subject of this chapter. Here, the cross slide leadscrew is first disengaged, allowing the cross slide movement to be controlled by a slideway mounted on the rear of the bed. This slideway may be set at an angle to the bed, so that as

the saddle moves along, the cross slide and turning tool are moved across, thus creating the taper. The design proposed here, features a slideway which measures over 300mm in length, so it becomes possible to achieve very accurate angular settings. For some industrial lathes where disengaging the leadscrew may be problematic, then a variation on the theme can involve adding a secondary cross slide, which then moves under the control of the attachment.

Much of the inspiration for the device proposed here came from an article published in *Model Engineer, Vol 200, No 4318,* by Mr Graham Howe. He employed setting registers 10 inches apart, which allowed extremely accurate positioning of the slide by using spacers. In some respects, the design presented lacks the professionalism of Mr Howe's, but for the less well equipped enthusiast who may have to beg or cajole the use of additional facilities, that given here should be somewhat easier to put together.

DESIGN AND CONSTRUCTION

As with many of my projects, the initial "design" phase started with a handful of sketches in the left hand, leaving the right hand free to pick among the contents of the scrap box.

The first item to be considered was the main support bracket which will be bolted to the rear of the bed. As supplied, the Mini-Lathe has a sheet metal splash back retained by a number of M5 screws into tapped holes in the rear face of the bed. Two of these are conveniently positioned and have been replaced by short lengths of M5 threaded rod, to support the bracket. Adding the threaded rod will avoid causing wear to the tapped holes in the bed.

I have suggested a 330mm length of 80mm x 40mm rectangular hollow section (RHS) for the bracket, because I had a piece slightly over this size to hand. Many other arrangements would equally suit, such as angle cut to a similar size, or even a fabrication. The basic requirement is to bolt to the bed and present a horizontal top surface to support the main assembly.

The swing plate is a length of 2in. x ½in. BMS flat (equivalent to cold-rolled steel). Again, it looked about right and was lying there silently shrieking "Please use me." A short 53mm piece of the same material forms the basis of the slide assembly. To minimize on machining, the dovetails are fabricated by bolting down strips of 20mm x 8mm BMS flat bar, the working faces being milled to 60 degrees.

The lengths were initially suggested by the spacing of the two tapped mounting holes in the bed. However, the long dovetail was shortened back a little to allow this to be machined in the Myford VMC mill. The reduction to 318 mm meant that the cutter could be maneuvered around to the second side without disturbing the work.

You could, of course, machine the dovetails in the best tradition of "hewn from the solid." I have chosen a bolted assembly, which cuts down on swarf generation. Using countersunk Allen screws gives a repeatable precision

location, provided that good quality screws are used. Mine come from Unbrako. Clearly, if you fit low quality screws whose heads are not accurately concentric, then the precision and repeatability of the assembled dimensions will suffer.

The swing plate is supported by two pairs of cross bars, each pair being spaced at 10.5mm. This arrangement gives a slot effect but without the need to cut the slots.

MANUFACTURE

I decided to first cut most of the material **(Photo 5.01)**, some of which needed a bit of attention to remove rust. Also at this stage, run a file along the faces of the pieces of flat bar to flatten out any damage marks along the corners.

BOX ANGLE (FIG 5.1)

The length of surplus material was first given a bit of de-rusting treatment, then cut to 330mm long. Before proceeding further, measure the distance between the mounting holes on the rear of the bed. In my case, this was slightly over 300mm. On one 40mm side of the box, two matching holes are drilled clearance for M5. In line, on the other side, two holes are drilled 13mm, then opened up

5.01 *Principal items of material for taper attachment*

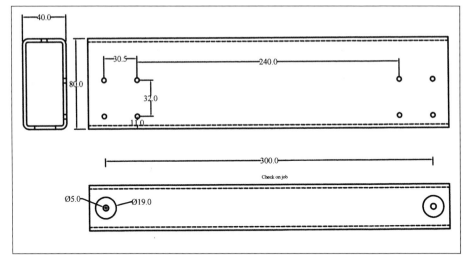

Fig 5.1 *Box angle*

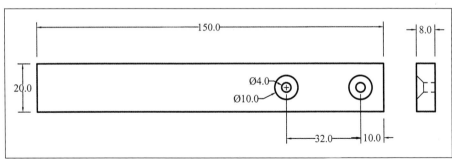

Fig 5.2 *Cross bar*

5.02 *Box angle bracket showing access holes for nut runner*

5.03 *M5 threaded rod avoids wear to tapped hole in bed*

5.04 *Box angle assembled with cross bars*

Fig 5.3 *Short dovetail*

a little further to accommodate the barrel of a nut runner **(Photo 5.02)**.

This hole is required because I had decided to fit two short lengths of M5 threaded rod in the holes **(Photo 5.03)**. Fitting the nuts this way would make mounting the device an easy and quick exercise. It then remained to drill and tap M4 the hole patterns to take the cross bars **(Fig 5.2)**. **Photo 5.04** shows the cross bars assembled to the box bracket.

It may be useful to consider to what extent any inaccuracies in this component may have on the final results. The top surface of the box may depart from horizontal as measured either along or across the bed. If we consider a height deviation of 1mm along, then, using Pythagoras, this can be translated into a horizontal length error of under 2 thousandths of a millimeter. Similarly it can be shown that deviation in crosswise height will also have little effect on work.

SHORT DOVETAILS (FIG 5.3)

These would each need one face milled as a dovetail working face. This could be done using a 60-degree dovetail cutter, but this

5.05 *Vise is sighted against protractor*

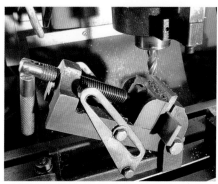

5.06 *Dovetail face cut with regular end mill*

is a costly item, and so I reserved its use for the long dovetail. An angle vise was set up by sighting against a protractor **(Photo 5.05)**, so that the edge might be cut back with a regular end mill **(Photo 5.06)**. On all the dovetail components, I have chosen to leave

5.07 *Un-machined land is visible*

an unmachined land of some 1.5mm, which can be seen in **Photo 5.07**. This land gives a bit of meat for the vise to grip on, should this be necessary.

SWING PLATE (FIG 5.4)

As I noted earlier, the material here had suffered at the hands of the tinworm. As one surface would become a dovetail contact face, I chose to shortcut by cleaning up the two wide faces on the surface grinder. If you do not have access to one of these, do not worry. Do, however, run a file gently over the surface to ensure there are no high spots, and clean off any rust by rubbing evenly with abrasive. The thickness of cold-rolled steel flats is likely to be sufficiently consistent for our purposes.

The work was then mounted on the mill table, ensuring it was lined up by pushing back against a pair of alignment pins. The line of mounting holes for the long dovetail was then spotted at 60mm spacing, this being read

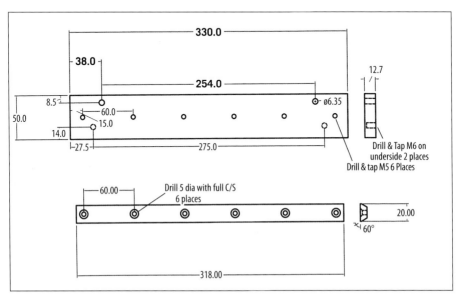

Fig 5.4 *Long dovetail*

from the DRO. I then drilled the holes through ¹¹⁄₆₄in. and tapped M5, and as there would be several, I set up the Tapmatic to speed things up. Two holes were drilled through and reamed ¹⁄₄in. for the setting pins **(Photo 5.08)**, and finally two were drilled from the underside. To avoid breaking through, the depth was set at ⁷⁄₁₆in. using a convenient drill shank **(Photo 5.09)**. These holes were then tapped M6 to

5.08 Reaming hole for setting pin

5.09 Preparing to tap a blind hole on the underside

take threaded rod for clamping. As the photos indicate, I carried out these last operations after assembling the slide. However, it would probably be more efficient to deal with these features at this stage.

LONG DOVETAIL BAR (FIG 5.4)

This too was set up on the mill and the holes spotted. I used a 10mm spotting drill **(Photo 5.10)**, taken to a depth which would also serve as the countersink for the M5 screws. I then drilled through 5mm diameter. Note that if you do not have the luxury of a DRO, make the dovetail bar first, then clamp in place on the swing plate, and spot through with a 5mm drill, before finally drilling and tapping.

To mill the long dovetail, the bar is first bolted down to the swing plate, with washers to introduce a small gap between the parts, as can be seen in **Photo 5.11**. The reason for this is that, when milling the 60-degree edges, the underside of the cutter can be kept clear of the swing plate, ensuring that only the inclined edges of the cutter are engaged. Bolting the relatively slender bar to the swing plate creates a rigid assembly which can more easily be clamped to the table and accurately machined.

I chose to push the assembly back against a pair of pins which match the size of the Tee slots, thereby ensuring that the work lines up with the table X axis **(Photo 5.12)**. Because I was a bit tight for table travel, some care was needed in positioning the work, ensuring that at one end, the cutter centerline just cleared the bar, and at the other, the cutter cleared sufficiently to be moved across to the second side.

After completing the first side, I added three more clamps **(Photo 5.13)**, two to act as stops and the third to add central hold down. Taking care to avoid disturbing the work, I repositioned the clamps at the ends and

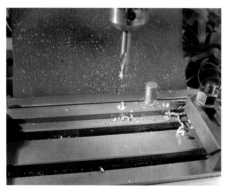

5.10 *Using a spotting drill on the long dovetail bar*

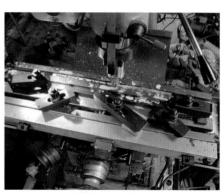

5.13 *Clamps added and stop pins removed to clear cutter*

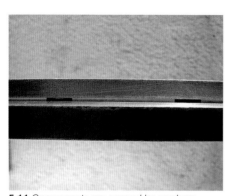

5.11 *Components are spaced by washers*

5.14 *Width is checked at several places over rollers*

5.12 *Milling the first side of the long dovetail*

removed the Tee slot pins to allow the cutter to progress along the second side.

After cutting side two, I checked the size for consistency at several points by means of a micrometer measuring over a couple of ¼in. diameter rollers, as in **Photo 5.14**. I then removed the spacing washers.

SLIDE ASSEMBLY

The slide base **(Fig 5.5)** was drilled 5mm diameter in four places. One of the short dovetails was then clamped in place and two holes spotted through. These were then

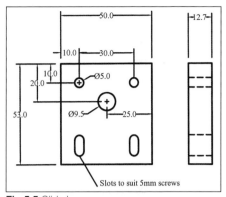

Fig 5.5 *Slide base*

5.17 *Slide bar assembly upper view, shims just visible between short dovetail and slide base.*

5.15 *Slide gripped in vise*

5.16 *Drilling slide base*

drilled through ¹¹⁄₆₄in. and tapped M5. I then bolted this first dovetail firmly in place.

It was then placed over the swing plate assembly, with the second short dovetail in position. The whole setup was then gripped in a vise, as shown in **Photo 5.15**, and the second pair of holes drilled down sufficiently deep to spot through to the upper surface of the second short dovetail. This was released, drilled through and tapped M5, while the two holes in the slide base were elongated to allow a little movement of the second short dovetail.

The whole thing could then be assembled. I employed hand pressure to squeeze the dovetails together while the bolts were tightened. It could then be checked for fit. I found that initially there was a tight spot about halfway along.

The remedy took two phases. First, a pointed triangular scraper took away metal at visible bright high spots. This was followed by the application of some fine-grade valve grinding paste to the inclined dovetail faces. After the slide had been worked along a few times and readjusted, the effort was rewarded by smooth, shake-free travel from one extreme to the other. I then cleaned and re-oiled the

5.18 *Slide bar assembly lower view*

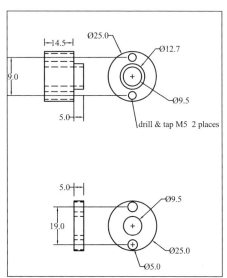

Fig 5.6 *Pillar*

slide. It would of course be very easy to increase the component count by two with a few screws and thus add a conventional "gib" adjustment feature. This has not however been found necessary.

My intention is that the slide should contact on the two outer horizontal faces, with slight clearance in the center. This clearance may be introduced by a number of methods such as 1) Mill away say a 0.25mm deep groove in the underside of the slide base plate, 2) Mill or grind away the same from the top of the long dovetail, or 3) Add thin shims between the short dovetails and the slide base plate. I have chosen the last option, using thin card on the basis that it will be easiest for the novice.

The hole is drilled ⅜in. in diameter **(Photo 5.16)** for the vertical pin, which will transmit the motion. The procedure adopted was to drill ²³⁄₆₄in. then ⅜in. which ensured a neat fit for a Loctited assembly, the pin being ⅜in. diameter drill rod cut to 43mm in length. **Photos 5.17** and **5.18** show the completed slide assembly upper and lower views.

The hollow pillar **(Fig 5.6)** was turned from two slices of 25mm steel bar. Drilling the central hole followed the sequence noted

5.19 *Drilling and tapping the pillar*

above. This would ideally be reamed for a close fit, but the two-stage drilling (perhaps my drill is a little worn on OD, but accurately ground) gave an acceptable result in the lathe. It was then transferred to the mill **(Photo 5.19)** to drill and tap the holes for the clamp screws. You could, of course mill two flats

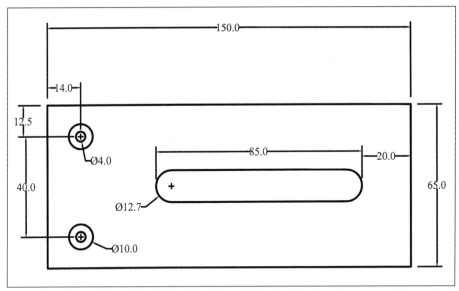

Fig 5.7 *Link plate*

(½in. across the flats, or AF) instead of turning down the ½in. diameter feature, which would certainly give a more professional feel and appearance to this component. Nevertheless, if you are making it on your Mini-Lathe, then the arrangement, as drawn, will be faster and easier to manufacture.

LINK PLATE (FIG 5.7)

This part functions to transmit the motion between the cross slide and the dovetail slide. It is held to the cross slide by two M4 countersunk screws, and has a milled half inch wide slot **(Photo 5.20)** to allow adjustment of the pillar position as may be required for different work diameters and turning tool arrangements. As may be seen from the **photos 5.20** and **5.21** plus **Fig 5.7**, it has been left in basic rectangular form. The aesthetics might be enhanced by trimming the sides to taper inwards towards the rear.

5.20 *Milling the slot in the link plate*

5.21 *Link plate and pillar assembled*

5.22 *Two holes are drilled and tapped in the cross slide*

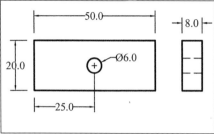

Fig 5.8 *Clamp plate*

Photo 5.21 shows the trial assembly of link plate and pillar.

MOD TO CROSS SLIDE

Two holes are drilled and tapped to secure the link plate. Depending on the kit available, you may choose to clamp the link plate in place with an overlap of about 28mm and spot through before drilling and tapping. Alternatively set up in the mill as shown in **Photo 5.22**.

CLAMP PLATES

Shown in **Fig 5.8** these are simply a couple of 50mm lengths of 20 x 8 CRS, each with a single central 6mm dia hole. They are mounted on lengths of M6 threaded rod and clamp the swing plate to the cross bars.

OPERATION

Before rushing forth into using the thing, it may be worth making a few observations on setup and calibration. There are two sources of potential error. First, in making the attachment, it is possible that a slight inaccuracy has been introduced in the positioning of the setting pins with reference to the dovetail slide. Second, we are dealing with a budget lathe, and therefore should be prepared to check its alignment if high precision work is to be undertaken.

There will be several ways by which work may be supported.

1) Rigid work held only in the chuck

2) Long work held in the chuck and supported by the tailstock center

3) Long work supported between centers

In each of these situations, opportunities for error can arise which will call for care in preparation or correction by calibration. Taking case (3) first, the Mini-Lathe, like most others, has provision for tailstock adjustment. A parallel bar may be set up between centers and the tailstock set so that it can be confirmed to line up correctly with the lathe axis using a dial test indicator (DTI). The taper attachment may then be assembled, set to zero by means of identical spacers at each setting pin and clamped up.

A DTI may then be set up on the toolpost and with the cross slide leadscrew disconnected, the carriage may be moved to the extremes allowed by the attachment, and the DTI reading checked. If the reading shows some deviation. Then either make a note and add this amount to the spacer at the appropriate end when turning tapers, or turn a new setting pin so that its altered diameter will zero the error. It is likely that the positions of the setting pins are not exactly equally offset from the long dovetail.

With an industrial toolroom quality machine, one would be confident that the spindle axis would be perfectly in line with the bed. This, however, is very much a budget machine and, for the price charged we just cannot expect the same degree of precision. In Chapter 2 of *Mini-Lathe*, I noted that on checking

5.23 *Setting using ¼in. plate to give the correct difference*

5.24 *Top slide set over about 25 degrees.*

the headstock alignment a very slight misalignment was present.

If you wish to turn tapers such as MT3 mounted in the chuck, as in case (1), then you need to check out your machine, determine if any error exists and adjust the taper setting accordingly.

Case (2) is likely to behave in a similar manner to case (1), except that if a good length of material is gripped in the chuck, then any slight misalignment, coupled with the supporting influence of the tailstock, would tend to cause infinitesimal bending of the work.

It must also be noted that most of the tapers we wish to cut are likely to be Nos. 2 and 3 Morse, those for Jacobs chuck arbors, and perhaps for ER collets. These are all relatively short, and should not give rise to significant accuracy problems.

FIRST TRIAL

I elected to do an initial test run, aiming to produce a No.2 Morse taper. I faced and centered a length of 19mm diameter bar. It could then be held in the three-jaw chuck and steadied by the tailstock center. After preparing the work, I removed the cross slide nut.

For this taper, my trusty Zeus book gives the small end diameter as 0.572in. and the end of socket diameter as 0.700in. with the taper per foot as 0.5994in. As the setting pins are pitched at 10in. apart, this latter figure was first scaled accordingly then halved to give a setting figure of 0.24975in.

The setting was achieved by using some "old technology": milling spacers of three inches each, with a piece of ¼in. flat added at one end **(Photo 5.23)**. I checked the turning tool for height, set roughly for position, the topslide being set to about 25 degrees **(Photo 5.24)**, and the pillar clamped to the link plate.

5.25 *The proof of the pudding*

Tool infeed, between cuts, would then be via the topslide.

To be better assured of a good finish, you could, of course, engage the power feed. However, my machine was set up for screwcutting 1mm pitch, and so I elected to feed manually. This was done by applying a little left-handed pressure to the carriage handwheel, while keeping a fairly consistent feed rate by using the right hand to turn the leadscrew handwheel. This, perhaps unorthodox, approach worked well and in a very short space of time the taper had been machined. The proof of the pudding **(Photo 5.25)** was to take the work out of the chuck, load it into the tailstock socket, and enjoy the satisfaction of a tight, shake-free fit.

On the basis of initial experience, I would now add a couple of further components. In the best traditions of Murphy's Law, swarf found its way into the holes vacated by the leadscrew retaining screws. A pair of small blanking plugs will prevent this and keep things clean in readiness for re-mounting the nut. Alternatively, those more pressed for time might just cover the area with a short length of sticky tape.

CHAPTER 6
LEVER FEED FOR THE TAILSTOCK

As the Mini-Lathe is a small-size machine, it is to be expected that the threads of the various leadscrews will be relatively fine. The 1.5mm pitch of the tailstock screw gives, on the one hand, fine control of depth, but on the other, many turns of the handle for any significant depth. Also, when working with

6.01 *Sensitive drilling attachment supplied by Myford*

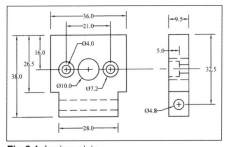

Fig 6.1 *Anchor plate*

very small drills, it can be helpful to be able to feed by a more sensitive means.

Myford offers an excellent accessory to give this sensitivity and their device is shown in **Photo 6.01**. It fits into the MT2 tailstock taper and thus can be used in conjunction with the regular screw feed. For drilling small-sized holes it can be a real boon. A lever feed also makes life so much easier if a small hole is to be drilled to relatively great depth, as it can so easily be "pecked" to clear the swarf.

The device offered here has been made as simple as possible, and is installed in place of the existing handwheel. The existing barrel and screw are left in place, thus catering for taper ejection, and giving a fine depth limit adjustment. The manufacture of the gadget is straightforward, with little need for precision. Close tolerances are not mandatory, but it is necessary to make matching pairs of parts and to make the aluminum anchor plate match the lathe. The dimensions given on the drawings are metric, but the raw material was very much imperial, hence the somewhat odd figures which result.

ANCHOR PLATE (FIG 6.1)

The material used here was ⅜in. aluminum. Feel free to use steel, but I find aluminum to be easier to work and, more importantly, it had some suitable offcuts. The work is

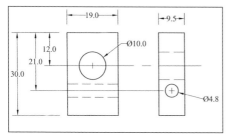

Fig 6.2 *Pressure block*

6.02 *Anchor plate*

6.03 *Pressure block*

first cut roughly to size then squared up and trimmed in the lathe, using the four-jaw chuck. The three holes in line (two 4mm counterbored and one 10mm) then need to be set out accurately so that the plate can be bolted on to the rear of the tailstock casting, and the main screw will pass through it.

How you achieve this will depend entirely on the kit at your disposal. It can be done on a mill with DRO, or on the Mini-Lathe using the milling attachments described in my *Mini-Lathe* book, or by removing the relevant part from the lathe, clamping to the plate, sighting to a scribed line and spotting through with 4mm and 10mm drills respectively.

Counterbores should ideally be cut with flat bottoms. However, for low stressed applications, I frequently cheat and simply drill down with a suitable jobber drill.

The next step was to cut the two-step features, and again this may be a cut and file operation, or carefully milled to size. It then remains to drill the ³⁄₁₆in. dia. hole for the pivot pin. The completed part is shown in **Photo 6.02**.

PRESSURE BLOCK (FIG 6.2 AND PHOTO 6.03)

This time a short piece of ³⁄₈in. x ³⁄₄in. aluminum flat bar, is cut then squared to size in the lathe. Two holes are then needed, one at 10mm dia. the second ³⁄₁₆in. dia. It may be found beneficial to file a few thousandths off the width to ensure free movement between the handle arms.

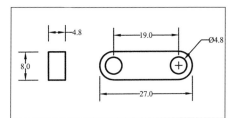

Fig 6.3 *Link*

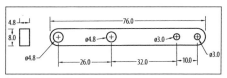

Fig 6.4 *Handle arm*

6.04 *Links and pivot pins*

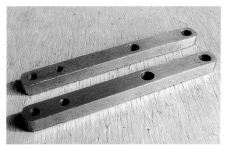

6.05 *Handle arms*

LINKS (FIG 6.3 AND PHOTO 6.04)

Two links are needed, and these were made from ³⁄₈in. x ³⁄₁₆in. rectangular CRS flat. The essential feature is that the center distance of the two holes is equal in both cases, and the solution is to cut roughly to size, drill one hole in each, pass a pin through both, clamp together and drill the two second holes in a single operation. After this, the ends may be tidied up by filing/ linishing to a radius.

HANDLE ARMS (FIG 6.4 AND PHOTO 6.05)

The philosophy here mirrors that for the links. The actual hole position is not critical, but the two parts should have identical hole spacing.

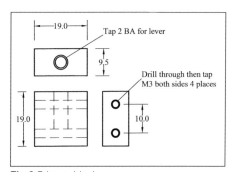

Fig 6.5 *Lever block*

LEVER BLOCK (FIG 6.5 AND PHOTO 6.06)

If you are relying on the "spot through" technique, then mark the positions of the two M3 holes using a 3mm drill through one of the arms. Then drill through 2.5mm dia and tap M3 in two places from each side. Next drill and tap the 2BA position for the lever. Note

Fig 6.6 *Lever*

that I used 2BA as I did not have an M5 die to hand for the lever. This hole should also be counterbored ³⁄₁₆in. diameter to a depth of some 2mm to clear the thread runout on the lever.

LEVER (FIG 6.6)

There is nothing dramatic here, just a length of 8mm BMS bar, cut to length, faced, turned down and threaded 2BA, then radiused at the outer end for comfort and appearance.

6.06 *Lever block*

KNOB (FIG 6.7 AND PHOTO 6.07)

This part basically fits in place of the tailstock handwheel, taking the "pull back" force from the pressure block. Mine was turned from a convenient piece of brass hex, then cross drilled and tapped to take an M3 setscrew for clamping.

6.07 *Knob showing position for setscrew*

PIVOT PINS (FIG 6.8 AND PHOTO 6.04)

Two are required made from ³⁄₁₆in. dia CRS. I have chosen to retain these two pins by 3.2mm (⅛in.) E clips. To achieve a neat fit, first measure the thickness of the E clips. Mine were 0.5mm. The cumulative thickness of the components (links, arms, block) is 1.5in. or 38.1mm, so the ideal positioning of the two grooves will be such that the inner faces of the clips are just over 38.1mm apart, and hence the measurement between the outer faces of the grooves will be just over 39.1mm.

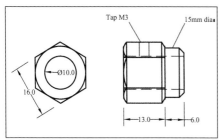

Fig 6.7 *Knob*

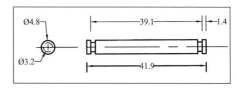

Fig 6.8 *Pivot pin*

The grooves may be cut with the inverted part off tool described in Chapter 7 of the *Mini-Lathe* book. Ideally, a blade should be ground to produce a groove just wider than the clips, but it is quite possible to use something wider. Before proceeding, measure the width of the part off blade; in my case, this was 1.6mm and the settings that follow are based on this blade width.

The rods were first faced to 41.9mm length. One was then located but not gripped in the three jaw chuck, with 7mm protruding. The tool was brought close to the work and the half nuts closed. The saddle was then moved using the leadscrew handwheel to contact the work, pushed back until a zero mark came round on the wheel. The chuck was tightened and the cross slide and tool retracted clear of the work. The leadscrew handwheel was employed to move the tool 3mm closer to the chuck.

The lathe was then started (in reverse) and the tool moved in to touch. The DRO handwheel could then be zeroed, and the groove cut accurately to a depth of 0.032in. taking the root diameter to ⅛in. for the E clip. This procedure was repeated for the second end and the second pin.

An alternative approach to setting the groove position is first to grip the work, bring the tool in close to the diameter of the work, then maneuver along so that the outer edge of the tool is level with the end of the work (as checked with a magnifying glass). Then move the tool along just 1.4mm to bring the groove edge to the desired location.

REMOVABLE PIN (FIG 6.9 AND PHOTO 6.08)

It is necessary that one pin be removable in order to access the screws to mount the

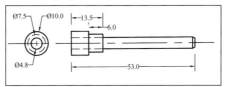

Fig 6.9 *Removable pin*

6.08 *Removable pin*

device on the lathe. Not drawn, this pin is a simple 53mm length of ³⁄₁₆ BMS rod, fitted with a turned brass head 13mm long retained by Loctite. The end of the pin has been lightly chamfered to facilitate fitting. If the device were to be used in a production setting, then I would recommend some means of keeping the pin in place. This might take the form of a cross drilling with a cotter pin, or perhaps a short thread with nut. For my occasional use, this embellishment has not been needed.

ASSEMBLY AND USE

The existing tailstock handwheel and nut are removed, followed by the leadscrew bearing and the leadscrew. The anchor plate sub assembly **(Photo 6.09)** is then fitted carrying the links and lever assembly, and the leadscrew refitted. The pressure plate is fitted over the leadscrew and the removable pin fitted. The knob is then added, along with

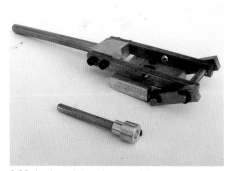

6.09 *Anchor plate sub assembly*

6.10 *Device fitted to Mini-Lathe*

the original handwheel retaining nut, these being set to allow free rotation of the screw. **Photos 6.09 and 6.10** show the device in an unfinished state (links and arms are rough sawn to length) and, in the latter picture, it is being used to drill the add-on head for the removable pin. In operation, rotation of the knob will allow fine adjustment of the maximum depth, and also permit extraction of Morse taper fittings.

CHAPTER 7

MULTI-POSITION SADDLE STOP

A factory-made single position stop is available for the Mini-Lathe and, given its affordable price, it is simply not worth making one. However, both of my other machines are equipped with multi-position stops, and over the years I have found these to be a great advantage when making more than two or three of a component whose design incorporates multiple length features. I therefore decided to investigate the possibility of adding something similar to the Mini-Lathe.

In my *Mini-Lathe* book, I described adding saddle clamps as a precursor to undertaking milling work on the machine. For those who have added the front clamp, fitting this new accessory will be very easy, as it is designed to locate over the clamp and use the same two tapped holes in the saddle for attachment. For those who have not added the clamp, I would suggest that this be made too, as, without it, some packing (approximately 10mm) is likely to be needed to bring the mounting plate out clear of the saddle gear case, and to provide space to accommodate the spring housing.

DESIGN PHILOSOPHY

In the case of the Myford Sevens, possibly due to the gap bed and position of the gearbox, the factory-supplied stop system

7.01 *Myford multi-position stop is fitted to rear of bed*

is fitted to the rear of the bed **(Photo 7.01)**. However, the Colchester arrangement follows the more usual practice of locating it at the front between saddle and headstock.

With a straight-bed format, the Mini-Lathe also lends itself to this layout. Industrial multi stops often cater for five or six positions, and my initial measurements and sketches were indeed based on a five-position stop.

It is a requirement that the stop bars, having a greater length than that selected, should be able to pass the static stop body, and the consequence is that more stops means greater barrel diameter.

Looking at the size and position of the projection on the existing stop, it is just possible to utilize this in conjunction with a five-stop barrel with an overall diameter of 32mm. A small clearance exists for this, which might be increased by filing a generous chamfer on the lower edge of the clamp plate. If the original stop were to be modified by removal of the protruding bar stop, then it could well be possible to arrange a six-position barrel, but this was not investigated.

Three main components are then needed: a mounting bracket, pivot and a barrel. Additional parts will be the five adjustable stops (lengths of M4 threaded rod with lock nuts) and the detent arrangement (a ball bearing, spring and housing).

Regarding the detent arrangement, commercial devices of this nature frequently use a ball or plunger and spring system, accommodating these parts within the barrel. **Photo 7.02** shows the Colchester unit dismantled, while **Photo 7.03** illustrates a similar homemade version which fits behind the Colchester cross slide to give set diameters. In both of these, the detent plunger drops into a circular array of seats at the various locations. By housing the spring and ball in the mounting plate, it is possible to use the existing holes in the barrel for indexing, and thus simplifying the construction.

An alternative detent might be designed, using perhaps an external leaf spring engaging with slots on the barrel. This, however, would add to the complexity.

7.02 *Component parts of the device supplied for the Colchester Bantam and Chipmaster lathes*

7.03 *Homemade multi-stop for Colchester cross slide*

QUICK CHANGE TOOLPOST: A BRIEF DIGRESSION

When I was compiling the *Mini-Lathe* book, the factory-supplied quick change toolpost was unavailable. One has since been made available, and I made full use of it for this project. **Photo 7.04** shows this toolpost dismantled to illustrate the clamping mechanism.

Typically, three different toolpost arrangements are available for the machine: 1) the four way (which requires the use of shims to set the tool height), 2) the two way rocker post (on which curved rocker plates allow the

7.04 *Parts of the Mini-Lathe quick change toolpost*

7.05 *QC toolpost fitted to lathe, pipless facing is easily accomplished*

tool height to be varied without undue change in angle) and 3) the quick change, (which is supplied with three tool holders, each of which carries a screw height adjuster).

Others will disagree, but I have never been a great fan of the four-way post except for use on a capstan lathe, where the overall size, rapid accurate indexing, and production requirements make it a good choice. On smaller-sized machines, having three sharp tools pointing in various directions seems to invite unscheduled bloodletting.

The rocker-type post employs geometry similar to that used by Myford on their rear toolpost and the system certainly works well, although some care is needed to achieve an accurate setting, and just two tools can be loaded.

Having used the Dickson quick change system exclusively on my Colchester, I am pretty much sold on the general idea of individual quick change tool holders, and have made a simpler system for the Myford and Orac.

It is probably not fair to draw comparisons between the Dickson kit and that supplied for the Mini-Lathe. The price difference is considerable and, of course, you get what

you pay for. So the Chinese offering lacks the hardened and fine ground finish, but nevertheless does allow the tool height to be quickly and conveniently set. **Photo 7.05** shows the toolpost on the machine, and it can be seen that the work has been faced off with no discernible center pip.

One minor criticism concerns the general design, which relies on pulling the holder back against two inclined faces. If one is careless, then it is possible to clamp the tool holder slightly "off square" viewed in plan.

As supplied, the holders will admit tools of just over 10mm thickness. Two of my homemade tools fit perfectly, but I was also keen to try the Unisix tooling supplied by Myford. These tools have carbide tips, which feature six edges, ground in such a way as to reduce the cutting forces by comparison with many others. The tool shanks are 11mm deep so I indulged in a little judicious butchering (angle grinder and file) to open up one holder to take one of these tools. When compared to the other tools, each of which carried an industrial type tip with noticeable nose radius (which would increase the cutting length and hence load), the cut was quieter and the finish better.

BARREL (FIG 7.1)

I cut a piece of steel bar, 32mm diameter and about 28mm long. At this point you may wish to start with a slightly longer piece to give more space should you wish to add a section of knurled surface. I cut mine to length and then, having decided to knurl as an afterthought, found myself tight on

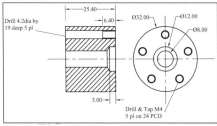

Fig 7.1 *Barrel*

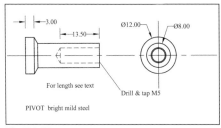

Fig 7.2 *Pivot*

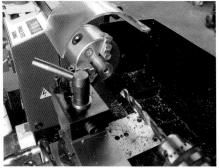

7.06 *Barrel has been faced and counterbored. Note this is the smaller 25mm barrel made for experiment.*

gripping length and clearance. To grip the work in the standard three-jaw chuck, the alternative jaw set was fitted. You might elect to machine away the outer surface of the bar for improved appearance, but I took a short cut and tidied up with emery.

I then faced at each end, drilled through 8mm, and finally counterbored 12mm **(Photo 7.06)** using a standard jobber drill with 118-degree point. In professional circles, this would probably be followed by cleaning out square with either a boring bar or drill ground flat. As this is a beginner's project, I have tried to simplify matters by profiling the pivot to match the counterbore, rather than add a square shoulder. The depth of counterbore is given as 3mm but no great accuracy is needed, as the pivot will be made to match.

Knurling, not detailed on the drawing, may be added at the counterbore end to give improved grip in service. The part is then put to one side for further attention.

PIVOT (FIG 7.2)

The raw material this time was 12mm diameter cold-rolled steel bar. Before loading the material, I set the turning tool to the required angle, by sighting it against one lip of a drill held in the chuck **(Photo 7.07)**. The diameter was reduced to 8mm for a little more than the length needed, and checked using the bore of the barrel to achieve an easy shake-free fit. On things like this, I often turn down to within about 0.1mm and then finish to size with a smooth file. I then formed the outer diameter, just under 12mm. The barrel could then be fitted over the work and checked for length.

One point to note is that ideally the turning tool should have a sharp corner. If it has a significant corner radius, then the radius left on the work will become the area of contact, rather than the 118-degree conical face.

7.07 *Tool tip is set to match the angle of the drill lip*

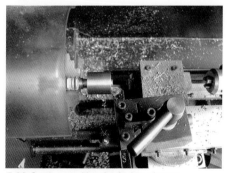

7.08 *Setting position for facing pivot to length*

When it is assembled, we aim to have a thousandth or two clearance between the barrel and the mounting bracket, this being achieved by the correct length of pivot. The turning tool is brought up to contact the barrel, which has been placed over the pivot **(Photo 7.08)** then backed off about 0.05mm (0.002in.). The barrel is then removed and the pivot faced at this setting. The final operation is to drill tapping size for M5 (I use ¹¹⁄₆₄in.) and use the tailstock chuck to start the tap on centerline. The work can then be transferred to the bench to hand tap the hole and saw off a little over length.

Back on the lathe, it is then faced to size at the head, before returning to the bench to add a screwdriver slot. Here I simply used a hacksaw. I then cut a length of M5 threaded rod so that, when screwed in, about 9.5mm protruded. I then Loctited this rod in place.

BACK TO THE BARREL

The headstock dividing attachment (described in *Model Engineers' Workshop* Issue 135 and the *Mini-Lathe* book) was set up with a 40-tooth change wheel in place, which would serve for the five positions **(Photo 7.09)**. The guided punch (discussed in

7.09 *Headstock dividing attachment has been set up with 40 tooth change wheel*

Issue 138) was also assembled in the toolpost **(Photo 7.10)**. The punch point was first set at the periphery of the barrel, then moved inwards by about 4mm. The dividing detent was set at a known starting tooth, and the punch given a sharp tap to indent the face of the barrel. This was then repeated for each of the other four positions.

The barrel was then taken to the drill, where the five locations were drilled through 3.3mm (tapping size for M4) and drilled from the back ¹¹⁄₆₄ (4.3mm) to reduce the tapping length. Each of the holes was then tapped M4, and feeding the tap through the clearance hole helped to keep the tap in line with the work.

Photo 7.11 shows the completed barrel alongside a smaller prototype, which was not pursued. Prospective builders who wish to follow industrial practice may stamp on numerals to identify the five stops.

Five pieces of M4 threaded rod form the stop rods, and the lengths chosen will be influenced by the type of work undertaken. The depth of the barrel will allow adjustment of each rod over a range of about 22mm (⅞in.).

7.10 *Guided punch is used to mark locations for holes*

MOUNTING PLATE (FIG 7.3)

For this, I used a scrap box find: a piece of 10mm thick aluminum plate. This was first cut and filed to shape, then clamped against the saddle clamp and the positions of the mounting holes spotted with a drill. These were then drilled through and counterbored to accept the heads of the two Allen screws.

I had earlier taken measurements on the machine, and from these had laid out a proposed position for the barrel. This was then marked, center popped, drilled and tapped M5. The plate could then fitted over the saddle clamp and secured in place. One length of M4 threaded rod was screwed into one position of the barrel, which was then fitted, being held in place by the pivot. The saddle and saddle stop were moved along the bed to give "hammer clearance."

7.11 *The 32mm barrel (left) and a trial 25mm (right)*

I then rotated the barrel to align the M4 rod with the saddle stop, and poked a 3.3mm drill down the "upper and outer" barrel position **(Photo 7.12)**. The end of the drill could then be gently tapped with a small hammer to mark the position on the mounting plate.

7.12 *A drill is used to mark the position for the spring housing*

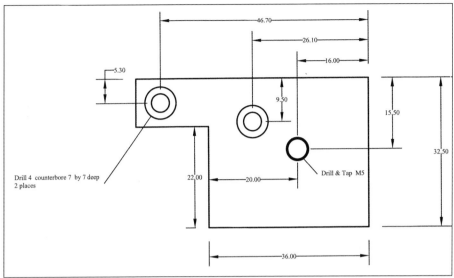

Fig 7.3 *Mounting plate*

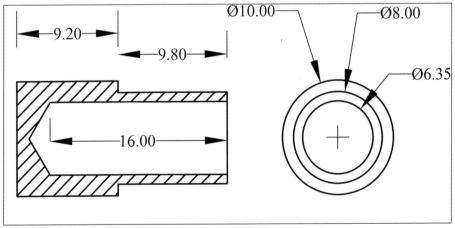

Fig 7.4 *Spring housing*

7.13 *Brass spring housing*

7.14 *Mounting plate with spring housing fitted, also ball and spring*

7.15 *Completed device fitted to lathe*

After it was dismantled, the plate was drilled through at this location, opening up to 8mm to take the spring housing.

DETENT PARTS SPRING HOUSING (FIG 7.4)

I used 10mm diameter brass bar here. The outer diameter was turned to just under 8mm diameter for a length of just under 10mm, and drilled some 16mm deep, opening up to 6.35mm (¼in.). It was parted off and faced to give an un-machined length just less than the thickness of the saddle clamp. This would ensure that the plate would locate squarely. The housing was then Loctited in the 8mm location hole in the mounting plate. The completed component can be seen in **Photo 7.13**.

SPRING AND BALL

The ¼in. (6.35mm) ball bearing was sourced as one from a pack at the local cycle shop. The spring was found in a job lot. The original dimensions were OD – 5.53mm, Length – 32mm, Wire diameter – 0.6mm. This was cut down to about 16mm (about 9 coils) so that, unloaded, the end of the spring sat nearly flush with the face of the mounting plate. The assembled mounting plate with housing is shown in **Photo 7.14**.

FINAL ASSEMBLY AND TEST

This is a bit of a fiddle, keeping the ball in place as the barrel is located. A smear of grease sufficed, and the device was successfully fitted, the result being shown in **Photo 7.15**. In the past I have come across multi stops, where, due to wear or perhaps dirt, the stop position was not sufficiently accurate to rely on for tight tolerance parts. To check on repeatability, I therefore set up a clock gage mounted on the saddle **(Photo 7.16)**, with the stylus arranged to contact the chuck face. Running the saddle against the

7.16 *Checking repeatability with a clock gage*

7.17 *Toolholder has been deliberately skewed for illustration*

7.18 *Measuring gap with drill*

7.19 *Modified tool holder now has projecting pin*

stop about ten times produced a series of readings, all within a thousandth. I judged, that for the kind of things I make, that's probably good enough.

POSTSCRIPT

The Quick Change toolpost could be mispositioned if carelessly fitted. **Photo 7.17** has been deliberately posed skewed to an extreme degree to illustrate this. After thinking about this, it occurred to me that the problem could be solved by an easy modification to the tool holder. First, lightly file the clamping faces to reduce high spots. Next, clamp the holder in place, taking care to position it correctly. Now measure the gap between holder and post. I used successively larger number drills, as in **Photo 7.18**. The holder is then drilled, say ⅛in. dia. by about ¼in. deep, (or 3mm dia by 6mm deep), and a short piece of suitable drill rod is Loctited in the hole. This is filed back so that it protrudes by an amount equal to the measured gap. **Photo 7.19** shows the result. When fitting, the holder is biased by hand so that the pin makes contact, thus improving positional repeatability.

CHAPTER 8
FOUR WAY TAILSTOCK TURRET

Over the years, several designs have been published for these accessories. The three that I found are listed below. In the past, casting kits were available for the Potts design, available from Woking Precision. Woking was taken over by Hemingway Kits, and I understand that they do plan to bring this accessory back into the range in the foreseeable future. Also, in recent years commercial versions have appeared from suppliers such as www.littlemachineshop.com.

The purpose of this gadget is to allow the setting of a number of tools which would normally be located directly in the tailstock, but in such a way that they may be brought into action more quickly, reducing changeover time. In an industrial situation, a capstan lathe, such as a Herbert or Ward, would allow, say, six tools to be arranged on the turret, which would auto index when retracted.

Capstan attachments are frequently available as accessories for center lathes, such as the Colchester Chipmaster or Student, and these usually substitute for the normal tailstock. The rapidity of tool change can have a dramatic effect on total machining time, when a significant batch is to be manufactured.

Turret accessories to fit the existing tailstock have been seen in several formats and are intended to take between three and six tools. Often the turret axis is inclined, so that, when not engaged, the tools swing up clear of the work. Sometimes, however, this geometry can lead to congestion due to the proximity of the saddle mounted toolposts. Having looked back over previously published designs, offered by Mr B Jackson in *Model Engineers' Workshop* Issue No 28 and intended for fitting to a Myford Seven, the horizontal axis arrangement seemed to offer much in the way of elegant simplicity, but might not work well if a rear toolpost were to be fitted. Given that many Mini-Lathes will be operated by relative beginners, this simplicity seemed a particularly relevant virtue and, as the Mini-lathe with standard cross slide is unlikely to be fitted with a rear toolpost, there is little likelihood of a foul in that area.

I have therefore taken the general layout of the Jackson design and adjusted sizes to suit the material readily available. Here, the turret axis is set parallel to the lathe axis (in a similar manner to many modern CNC machines), making construction considerably easier.

Only four major components are needed: the arbor, the bracket, the turret, and the pivot. The whole thing can be made with little need to measure to tight tolerances. There is no need for a milling machine, dividing head or rotary table. Certainly, some holes do need to be positioned accurately, but this can be achieved in some instances by spotting through, and in others by drilling *in situ* on the lathe. One point which I should mention, however, is that the tailstock alignment should be spot-on, as any error will affect the accuracy of the tool locations.

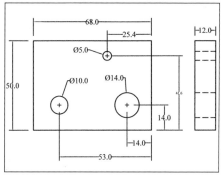

Fig 8.1 *Bracket*

BRACKET (FIG 8.1)

In my scrap box, I found a convenient piece of old imperial stock cold-rolled steel flat bar measuring 2in.by 0.5in. in section). I cut this to a length of 68mm. Moving into the 21st century, the modern equivalent would be 50mm x 12mm, as reflected in the drawing. I then coated the blank with marking blue before the positions for the three holes were marked out **(Photo 8.1)** and drilled.

Many drills cut slightly oversize, especially if they are inaccurately ground. To obtain an accurate drilled size, drill first through 0.5mm undersize, then follow through with the final size. A "Silver and Deming" drill was used for the largest size, as these drills are available in sizes over 0.5in. but have shanks of just that diameter, which conveniently fit the average drilling machine.

For positioning the holes, the old fashioned "scribe, center pop, start with a 1.5mm drill" technique was used, before drilling through and opening up to size. **(Photo 8.2)**. The position of each hole on this part does not need to be desperately accurate. A bit of error either way will not matter, as features on the disk are spotted through, and one automatically fits the other.

8.1 *Marking out the blued bracket*

8.2 *Drilling to size using a Silver and Deming drill*

DISK (FIG 8.2)

Here, my scrap box yielded a rusty, steel round blank somewhat larger and thicker than needed. I therefore took the liberty of roughing it down to size in the Chipmaster. This piece of steel was probably mild, but of unknown provenance. It certainly did not machine particularly cleanly, and I would recommend that other prospective builders use 12L14. If you start with a slice of 100mm (4in.) diameter bar, then it is straightforward to set up true in the four jaw **(Photo 8.3)** before facing to thickness, and drilling/ boring the central hole. Add a 1mm chamfer on one side of the hole. (The chamfer is intended to avoid interference with the small radius likely to be found on the pivot shoulder.). Again, no great attention to accuracy is needed, as the pivot will be turned to fit. The part is then set aside awaiting further operations.

PIVOT FIG 8.4

I used hex steel bar here, as the shape gives wrench grip with no further machining. However, round bar is a perfectly feasible alternative, though you may wish to file a pair of wrench flats later. The material is gripped in the three jaw, with about 30mm projecting. Next turn down the diameter for a length of about 27mm to give a close fit in the disk.

Now place the disk over the pivot (chamfered side to the chuck) and push hard up against the shoulder. With the saddle against its suitably positioned stop, employ the topslide to move the tool to just touch a 0.003in. (0.075mm) feeler gage sandwiched between tool and disk **(Photo 8.4)**. The disk is then removed and the next shoulder machined at that length setting to fit closely the 12mm hole in the Bracket. Center drill, and drill 5mm as preparation for the M6 thread, then tap.

At this stage it should be possible to trial assemble the disk and bracket. Nip up with an M6 screw and check that the disk can be rotated without undue play. If it binds, extend its location diameter by a couple of

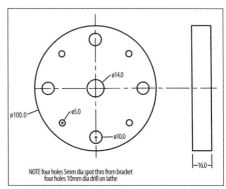

NOTE four holes 5mm dia spot thro from bracket
four holes 10mm dia drill on lathe

Fig 8.2 *Disk*

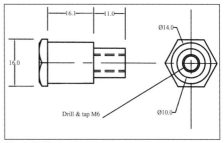

Fig 8.3 *Pivot*

8.3 Facing the disk

8.4 *Setting the tool position with feeler gage for shoulder length*

8.5 *Detail view of the screw in brass dummy tang*

8.6 *Arbor is located via a 3-2 reducer sleeve directly in lathe spindle*

thousandths. Finally, either saw or part off to length before reversing to face and chamfer.

ARBOR

A number two Morse taper is needed to locate the device in the tailstock. If you do not wish to machine one from scratch, then blank end arbors are available from many of our regular suppliers at surprisingly low cost. As it happened, I still had the piece machined with the correct taper, which had been used as an exercise for the taper turning attachment described in *MEW* Issue No 141.

Morse tapers usually have a tang, against which a drift will bear for extraction from a socket. Some arbors may be found with no tang but drilled and tapped for a draw bar. Mine was given this treatment, then fitted with a "screw in" tang made from a brass M10 setscrew **(Photo 8.5)**. With this in place, removal from a MT 2-3 adapter using a normal taper drift would not be a problem. The screw would also be left in place later for auto release from the tailstock. The arbor was fitted to the tailstock, to check the depth of engagement, and felt tip marks applied to indicate the rough axial position for the bracket location diameter.

With the normal chuck removed, the work was loaded into the headstock via an MT 2-3 adapter. The end was then turned down to closely fit the 14mm hole in the bracket, the length of this location diameter being slightly less than the thickness of the bracket. **Photo 8.6** shows this operation under way.

RETURN TO THE DISK

I scribed two perpendicular lines diametrically across the disk. Here I used the center finder made in the RR training center back in 1963 **(Photo 8.7)**. Again, due to the manufacturing sequence, no great precision is needed.

8.7 *Disk is scribed with two perpendicular diameters*

8.8 *Bracket and disk bolted up with washer, then holes are spotted through*

Now the disk, bracket and pivot are assembled, with a large washer sandwiched between disk and bracket. The disk is then rotated until one line can be seen centrally in the ³⁄₁₆in. hole. Holding this position, the bolt is tightened clamping the parts. A ³⁄₁₆in. drill was employed to spot through and drill, say, a couple of mm deep **(Photo 8.8)**. This process was repeated for the other three positions. The parts may then be dismantled and the four holes drilled through ³⁄₁₆in. diameter. I chose to use ³⁄₁₆in. as I had this size in my stock of drill rod – which would be used for the detent pin. For metric workers, I have suggested 5mm on the drawing but anything around this size should be satisfactory.

As a final operation, the disk and bracket were reassembled, and a toolmaker's reamer (shown in **Photo 8.9** and made from the same drill rod as the detent pin) was then gently fed though the pair in each of the four positions, giving a smooth fit for the pin, which is not drawn. Making it was a straightforward case of turning a brass knob, and Loctiting it to a short length of drill rod.

8.9 *Toolmaker's reamer is readily made from drill rod*

ASSEMBLY

The arbor is now Loctited to the bracket **(Photo 8.10)** and left to cure. The disk and pivot were assembled, bolted up, and the entire assembly fitted to the tailstock. The disk was rotated to one of the four positions, and the pin engaged. I then drilled a hole almost through the disk, using first a 9.5mm then a 10mm drill mounted in the three-jaw chuck. The setup can be seen in **Photo 8.11.** The work was then dismantled and the disk drilled through in the drill press.

The action of drilling the locations on the lathe ensures that each tool location will be accurately positioned on the lathe centerline and parallel to it.

I then took the disk to the drill press **(Photo 8.12)** where the four holes for tool holder clamp screws were drilled (positioned by eye), then tapped M4.

Finally, tool holders may be made to suit the equipment to be used. Two were quickly made for illustrative purposes shown in **Photo 8.13** along with the detent pin. These can be seen mounted on the machine in **Photo 8.14**, where the general arrangement of the device may be seen, here set up to center drill, then drill. Although the holders here have been made to near equal lengths, it may be advantageous to make some longer (e.g. for center drills)so that the total tool projection does not vary overmuch. Other tools which might be accommodated could include such as D-bits, flat-bottomed drills, countersink bits, and so on.

CONCLUSION

The design and manufacturing sequence has been set out with the Mini-Lathe and relative newcomer to the hobby in mind. Clearly, the method and sequence of manufacture may be very different if a milling machine with DRO and dividing head/ rotary table is to hand. One downside of the design is that if it is applied to, say, a Myford Seven, then it is most likely that a rear toolpost may not be used at the same time. If the long cross slide is made for the Mini-Lathe, then it opens up the possibility of a rear mounted toolpost (RTP). In that case, an inclined turret arrangement might be considered. Both of these projects are described in later chapters.

8.10 *Bracket is Loctited to arbor*

8.11 *Drilling disk in lathe ensures accurate tool position*

8.12 *Drilling holes for clamp screws*

REFERENCES TO ARTICLES IN MODEL ENGINEERS WORKSHOP

MEW Issue No 22 page 33 Harold Hall – a three way turret with inclined axis

MEW Issue No 27 page 59 B. Jackson – a four way device having a horizontal axis

MEW Issue No 78 page 48 Peter Rawlinson – a six-way, inclined axis design probably better suited to larger lathes, e.g. 5in. center height.

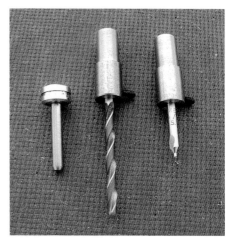

8.13 *Detent pin (left) with toolholders fitted with center drill and drill*

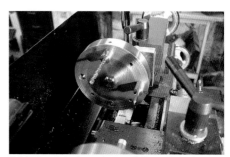

8.14 *Turret device setup on lathe with just two tools to center drill and drill*

CHAPTER 9

LONG CROSS SLIDE

With many small lathes, one aspect which frequently arises is the length and travel of the cross slide. As can be seen in **Photo 9.01**, if the slide is wound fully back, then a normally mounted tool tip will be at a radius of just an inch or so. This is not a problem if you work in small scales, but if like most model engineers you stretch your equipment to (or even beyond) its limits, then this project may offer an improvement.

The opportunity has also been taken, to thicken up the cross slide, (pinching thickness from other parts to maintain the tool height) which may open the way to adding T-slots. Certainly the added length will offer the facility to mount a rear toolpost.

One of the minor inconveniences encountered when setting/unsetting the Mini-Lathe topslide for angle work is that it needs to be wound back to access the two clamping bolts from above. One of the improvements featured on the Myford Super Seven over the earlier ML7 model is the means by which this operation is handled. The ML7 has two clamp nuts and studs, accessed from above. The topslide rotation is restricted. For the S7, clamping is accomplished by a pair of opposed screws acting on a circular tapered plug, which projects down into the cross slide. This arrangement is employed here and allows

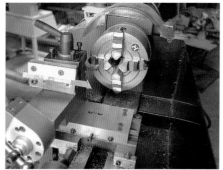

9.01 Standard cross slide shown wound fully back

(subject to clearance) full 360-degree rotation. For this project, you will need access to a sizeable milling machine, capable of handling the material.

I ordered a suitable lump of cast iron. Continuously cast bar is a material which can also be relied on as regards quality – unlike some castings, there are no blow holes or hard spots. As usual, I could not resist putting the cart before the horse, and starting to machine before detail designing, at least as far as cleaning up the cast iron was concerned.

To rip off the outer cast surface as quickly as possible, I set it up in an 8-inch vise on the Matchmaker. Although this is a CNC machine, it does have a facility for "manual move," which avoids the need to write a program. Simply jog to the start position and specify a move of say 300mm in X at a given feed rate, and off it goes, just like a conventional power traverse.

The cutter I employed was a six tip, three-inch diameter, facing type which would span the full width of the "plank." The sides and long edges **(Photo 9.02)** were dealt with. Due to slight variation of cutter tip projection, the surface finish left a little to be desired, hence the faces were treated to a tidy up on the surface grinder. **Photo 9.03** shows the lump looking quite pretty after grinding, alongside the original cross slide.

9.02 *A face mill used in the Matchmaker to square off the faces*

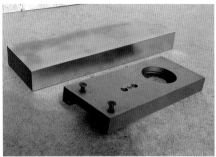

9.03 *Original slide shown against blank for the new*

I then measured up the existing cross slide and scribbled a few sketches of the revised version. The existing cross slide is fitted with a substantial gib strip, and here I felt that something a little thinner would suffice. Hence the new dovetail size, while fitting over the existing base, is slightly narrower than the original.

The correct size of counterbores for cap head Allen screws is a subject which crops up from time to time, and here I often adopt a somewhat cavalier approach and use a conventional jobber drill of appropriate size. This, of course, creates the disadvantage that the head beds on a conical rather than flat face, but unless the assembly is highly stressed it is unlikely to cause a problem. If tightened hard, then some plastic deformation will occur, and the bore may be moved inwards causing interference with the shank of the screw. An alternative approach, which I have utilized in this exercise, is to trim slightly the heads of the Allen screws to allow the use of a stock size of end mill for creating the counterbores. Thus, the screws used here were trimmed as follows: M4 to 6.3mm dia, allowing a ¼in. counterbore, M5 to 7.8mm for ⁵⁄₁₆in. or 8mm, and M6 to 9.4mm for ⅜in. dia.

MACHINING TO SIZE

After cleaning up, as described above, the plank measured about 68mm x 212mm x 25mm. The width and length were considered about right, but the thickness could be reduced, so it was taken down to 21mm. The material was then cleared for the dovetail by cutting a channel 6.6mm deep and 40mm wide, using a normal ¾in. endmill held in a Clarkson Autolock chuck **(Photo 9.04)**.

The cutter was then changed for the 60-degree dovetail **(Photo 9.05)** which was set first at a depth of 6.4mm and moved

9.04 *The bulk of the material is removed from the slot using an endmill*

9.05 *Starting to cut the dovetail angle*

across progressively to produce the angled face, followed by a final cut at the same Y setting, but with the depth increased to 6.5mm. This would then cut just on the horizontal face, which I believe gives a better finish. The opposite side of the dovetail was produced by repeating the sequence. The ¾in. endmill was finally used to square off the ends to 210mm **(Photo 9.06)**.

At this stage, while I had the bones of the design rattling around at the back of the brain, not a lot had been committed to paper, so the prototype slide was put to one side pending firming up on other details. These would include boring the hole for topslide location **(Photo 9.07)** with its attendant clamp screw positions and drilling/tapping the two holes to take the aluminum stand offs, also the holes for the gib strip adjuster and slide clamp screws. **Fig 9.1** gives the detail for the new slide.

GIB STRIP

This was certainly one of my "cart before horse" exercises, in that I had machined the dovetail to size before finally deciding on the gib material, whereas it would have been easier to work the other way round.

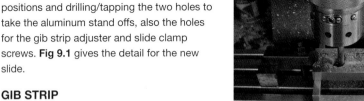

9.06 *Squaring off the end of the slab*

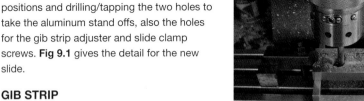

9.07 *The topslide location bore was finished with a boring head*

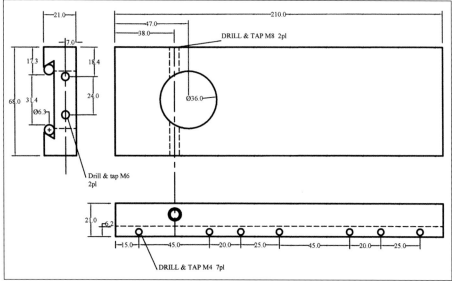

Fig 9.1 *Long cross slide*

My excuse stems from the likelihood (subsequently confirmed) that a strip of 13mm x 5mm hot-rolled steel strip would be used, as I had no suitable bright steel or brass to hand, and that this would be first "brightened up" and then reduced to thickness by surface grinding. The thickness could then be accurately adjusted to match the clearance. My suggestion to others would be to make this part first from a strip of perhaps 3mm or 4mm thickness (or at least decide on the material) then produce a dovetail to suit.

To cut the angled edges, the strip was set up in an angle vise, which unfortunately had a jaw width of only about 2.5in. The job was thus done in several stages, each reposition introducing the prospect of a small error. Fortunately, this does not cause a problem, just a little variable clearance above and below the strip when assembled. Once it had been

9.08 *To drill the screw positions, the gib strip was clamped in place using rod*

checked for fit, it was clamped to the new slide **(Photo 9.08)** to spot drill the positions for the points of the adjusting screws.

TOPSLIDE SPIGOT

Fig 9.2 shows the detail of this part, made from a length of 38mm free-cutting mild steel bar. **Photo 9.09** illustrates that part of the turning exercise where the 20-degree angled

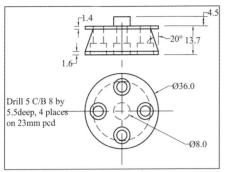

Fig 9.2 *Spigot*

9.09 *Initial work on the top slide spigot*

face is being cut. For speed, the metal was ripped down in the Chipmaster, although holding the reversed embryo part to produce the 8mm location spigot (which you might argue is not necessary) was then found to be easier in the Myford. **Photo 9.10** shows the operation to drill counterbores for the attachment screws.

LEADSCREW AND NUTS

Early on in the proceedings, I had decided that, for ease of manufacture, the leadscrew should be made from mild steel threaded rod. Settling on ⁷⁄₁₆ UNF would give 20 tpi, allowing compatibility with the DRO units supplied for the machine. It must be acknowledged that threaded rod is by no means a perfectly accurate thread; however the lead error is likely to be in the region of a thousandth or so per inch. Threaded rod quality does vary, so you should examine the thread form – some is distinctly truncated and not fully formed. It also pays to shop around. One local source quoted a price nearly three times that of another.

By using this material, machining the leadscrew is a simple matter of cutting to length, turning away unwanted thread **(Photo 9.11)** and creating a small keyway. The details are given in **Fig 9.3.** One point to note here

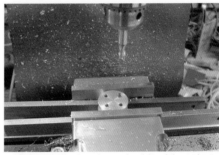

9.10 *Counterboring the underside of the spigot for the attachment screws*

9.11 *Turning down to 10mm removes much of the thread*

is that the setscrew which will engage in the keyway has a pointed end. I therefore chose to cut the keyway **(Photo 9.12)** with a ball-nosed cutter. As can be seen in this photo, a standard drill chuck was used, and while

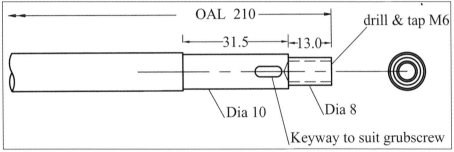

Fig 9.3 *Leadscrew*

this is not recommended practice for holding milling cutters, it can work reasonably well for light work.

The leadscrew nut might best be made from phosphor bronze. As none of this was to hand, I tried using a piece of moly loaded black nylon. I don't machine plastics frequently enough to acquire expertise, so the finish was pretty rough and the turning operation was interrupted several times to cut away swarf. The nut has been drawn as made **(Fig 9.4)**, again part of the cart pre-horse scenario. At the outset, I thought it might be possible to pass the body of nut into the cross slide base, but decided against this. As a result, the nut might be a simple cylindrical cheese featuring the necessary holes, with the upper segment cut away for clearance.

Two other ⁷⁄₁₆in. UNF nuts were made, both from 19mm AF brass hex material, and turned to a thickness of 9.5mm. One is Loctited in place on the screw behind the DRO assembly, while the second is fitted with an M4 setscrew and brass pad to allow adjustment of its position and hence screw endfloat.

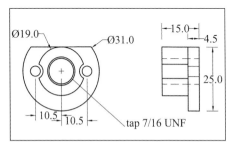

Fig 9.4 *Leadscrew nut*

9.12 *Keyway was cut with using a ball-nosed cutter*

9.13 *A short length of threaded rod is Loctited in each stand off*

9.14 *Bracket details were drilled before sawing the part away from the stock material*

STAND OFFS AND MOUNTING DETAILS

A total of six aluminum stand offs were made, all 50mm in length and 0.5in. in diameter. Two support the outer end of the leadscrew and DRO assembly, and the others carry and reposition the splash back. The pair associated with the screw assembly are drilled and tapped M6 at each end. A short length (about 20mm) of M6 threaded rod is then Loctited in place in one end of each stand off **(Photo 9.13)**. The others are treated in a similar manner but have M5 threads and rods. The attachment plate **(Fig 9.5)** was sawn from a piece of 38mm x 9.5mm aluminum flat bar, drilling being done while part of the larger lump **(Photo 9.14)**. This part might equally be made from steel. Note that the drop from top surface to leadscrew location has not been specified on the drawing. This was found to be 25.6mm, but my suggestion is to determine on the job, either by measurement, or by making up a short length of threaded rod with a sharp point, and sliding the assembly in to create a mark.

Attached to the plate is a circular steel spacer **(Fig 9.6)** which is screwed to the

9.15 *Drilling the circular steel spacer*

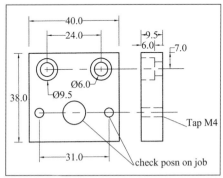

Fig 9.5 *Attachment plate*

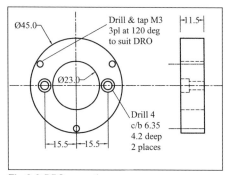

Fig 9.6 DRO mounting

[In figure: Ø45.0 / Drill & tap M3 3pl at 120 deg to suit DRO / 11.5 / Ø23.0 / Drill 4 c/b 6.35 4.2 deep 2 places / 15.5 15.5]

9.16 Completed spacer drilled, tapped and counterbored

9.17 Assembly of cross slide moving parts

bracket, and in turn carries the DRO head. Its manufacture is a straightforward exercise in turning, then drilling and counterboring the positions for the two attachment screws, and finally drilling and tapping three M3 locations for the screws which will hold the DRO in place. **Photo 9.15** shows drilling in progress, and **Photo 9.16** the finished part. The make up of the parts associated with the moving slide can be seen in **Photo 9.17**.

CLAMP SCREWS AND PADS

Clamping the topslide is accomplished by means of two M8 Allen screws, each fitted with a brass pressure pad to avoid bruising the spigot. Cutting the end of the pads to the correct angle involves a bit of guesswork with the hacksaw, followed by trial and error with the file. The end of one of the pads is just visible in **Photo 9.18**.

MODIFICATION TO TOP SLIDE

I noted earlier that at the outset it might have been necessary to reduce the height of the topslide to compensate for the thicker cross slide. If using the standard toolpost, this would probably be required. By using a quick change post, the toolholder can be locked in position a few millimeters below the topslide surface. However, this was possible only in the zero and 90-degree positions. **Photo 9.19** shows the topslide set up in the lathe to turn away the corners, and **Photo 9.20** illustrates the modified part. This allowed the QC toolpost to be mounted at any angle, as can be seen in **Photo 9.21**.

SWARF GUARD

Illustrated in **Fig 9.7**, this is cut from 18g or 1.2mm sheet steel. I happened to have a

9.18 *The tip of one brass pad is visible within the bore*

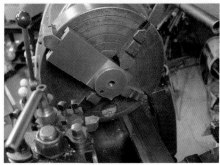

9.19 *Topslide set up for modification*

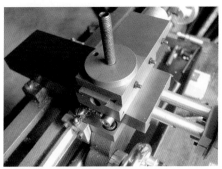

9.20 *Modified slide allows toolpost rotation*

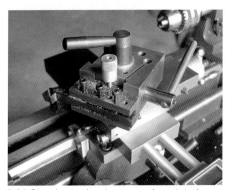

9.21 *Showing toolpost can now be rotated*

convenient piece of Galvatite, which is steel with a zinc galvanized surface, and is hence good for corrosion resistance (less so for paint adhesion). The drawing reflects what was made, but again, I suggest checking on the job. Two holes are shown at 52mm centers. You may choose to set these at 50mm matching the standoff length, but I suggest that these be elongated by filing to achieve optimum assembly.

Sheet steel is commonly available in at least three forms. Natural is bare steel, which is fine for welding, but obviously prone to rust. Zintec is a version with a form of zinc coating applied, and is regularly used for welded assemblies. The corrosion resistance is better than natural, but in my experience, not as good as Galvatite, the last being often used for H/V ducting. There are nowadays also a number of sheet steel products aimed at the building industry, where the finish may be painted.

Photo 9.22 shows the added guard fitted and the standoffs which move the main guard back a couple of inches to give the extra clearance needed for the long cross slide.

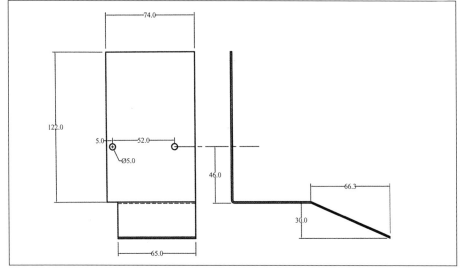

Fig 9.7 *Swarf guard*

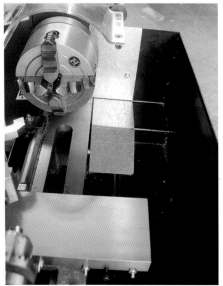

9.22 *View showing added guard and standoffs for main guard*

CONCLUSION

This exercise is one which will require the use of a mill and a lathe rather larger than the Mini-Lathe. However, for those able to access the required facilities, this mod does give the machine a capability/ convenience which stems from the added cross slide travel and the revised arrangement for swiveling the top slide. The added thickness probably paves the way to introduce T-slots, but at the time of writing, I have not pursued this point.

CHAPTER 10
FIVE WAY TAILSTOCK TURRET

BACKGROUND

In Chapter 8, I offered a simple design for a four way tailstock turret intended for, and able to be built upon, the Mini-Lathe. That design featured a disk turret which revolved on a horizontal axis. This arrangement is fine for the standard Mini-Lathe where the standard cross slide saddle does not allow space for a rear toolpost. Parting off is conveniently undertaken by using an upside down front tool and reverse rotation. However, this layout will not work within the confines of front plus rear toolposts commonly found on industrial and Myford machines.

Having found the four way gadget described earlier to be useful with the standard cross slide on the Mini-Lathe, I then set about concocting an alternative arrangement for my Myford. This may also be used on the Mini-Lathe, in conjunction with the long cross slide assembly, which was described in Chapter 9. To achieve a compact envelope, this design inclines the turret axis at 45 degrees to the spindle centerline, in a similar manner to the Potts six way turret which used to be available from Woking Precision, and which is expected to again become obtainable from new owners Hemingway kits.

Whereas the disk type device could be made entirely on a small lathe, I have built this

10.1 *Completed tailstock turret fitted to the Myford*

one using various lathes and a mill. At one stage the surface grinder was called in to play, but this should not be necessary. Apart from turning a couple of diameters to closely fit bores, no great accuracy should be needed. The turret tool locations are drilled on the lathe and their positions are thus automatically fixed to a good level of precision, provided the tailstock is correctly aligned.

Because the project evolved initially with the Myford in mind, most of the photos show this machine or the Colchester Chipmaster rather than the Mini-Lathe. **Photo 10.01** shows the device fitted to the Super Seven, and it can be seen that the design of the detent/latch should be considered as a work in progress. It works well, but might be made with different

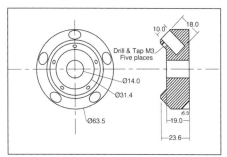

Fig 10.1 *Turret*

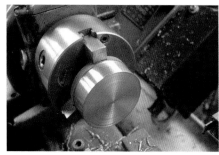

10.2 *Steel blank is cleaning up well*

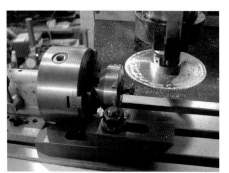

10.3 *Work held on an arbor to machine slots, as the 45-degree feature was cut prematurely*

10.4 *Boring the recess in the turret*

proportions for easier opening with thumb or finger. Although the general layout had been roughed out in CAD, the final design and manufacture moved forward in a somewhat haphazard sequence. With the benefit of hindsight, I have therefore suggested a slightly different sequence of operations for making the turret.

TURRET (FIG 10.1)

I cleaned up a rusty slice of free machining steel, then faced and turned to diameter and thickness **(Photo 10.02)**. It was then bored 14mm. I then proceeded to carve the angled face and recess, but this is best left till later, so that the work can be more easily held for milling.

I then used a 5in. diameter by ¹⁄₁₆in. thick slitting saw to cut the five slots for the detent positions. As can be seen in **Photo 10.03**, I mounted the work on a turned arbor and used a small dividing attachment, but in fact angular accuracy is not necessary. If you do not have dividing equipment, then just mark off with a protractor. If you are a bit out, it will simply mean that the tool locations will not be perfectly evenly spaced. Each tool will, though, be correctly positioned when engaged. The work was placed on the table

10.5 *Topslide is set over to 45 degrees to create conical features*

10.6 *Detail view of pivot*

so that the periphery of the saw would cut at about 45 degrees viewed in plan.

The work is then returned to the lathe. The recess can be bored 5mm deep by 31.4mm diameter **(Photo 10.04)**, then the topslide set over 45 degrees one way then the other to turn the conical faces **(Photo 10.05)**.

PIVOT (FIG 10.2)

The chosen material here was 19mm AF hexagon steel bar, again free machining. Two dimensions require care: the length and diameter of the location for the turret. The diameter needs to give smooth, shake-free rotation, and the length about 0.003in. greater than the thickness of the turret, so that the pivot may be tightened firmly while still allowing the turret to rotate. The completed pivot is illustrated in **Photo 10.06**.

Although not detailed on the drawing, it may be found useful to undercut slightly with a parting tool at each of the shoulders. This will avoid the thread binding at its runout before being screwed fully home and avoid interference if there is a significant radius under the head. (A consequence of tool tip radius.)

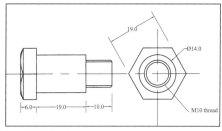

Fig 10.2 *Pivot*

BODY (FIG 10.3)

As can be seen in **Photo 10.07** this started life as a piece of **2.5in. x 1.0in.** cold-rolled steel flat, from which a piece was sawn off at 45 degrees. When machined, cold-rolled steel may distort due to internal stresses. **Photo 10.08** shows that this has indeed occurred here. The witness marks from a flat file demonstrate slight bowing along the surface.

The work was first set up in the mill to machine a second face at 90 degrees, then, using an adjustable square **(Photo 10.09)**, it was angled and gripped to cut the 45-degree side as shown in **Photo 10.10**.

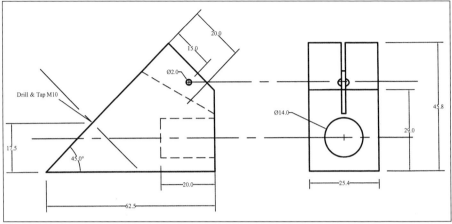

Fig 10.3 *Body*

10.7 *Material for the body is sliced off near to size in the bandsaw*

10.8 *File marks confirm that slight distortion had occurred*

10.9 *Adjustable square used to set 45-degree angle*

10.10 *Cleaning up the angled face with a "Little Hogger" tool from Chronos*

10.11 *Drilling the location hole for the arbor*

10.12 *Tapping the hole for the pivot*

10.13 *Cutting off the unwanted corner*

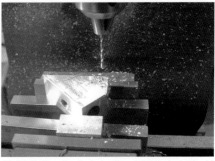

10.14 *Drilling the hole for the detent pivot pin. Note block of aluminum avoids vise damage to corner.*

Two holes are then drilled, the first for the arbor **(Photo 10.11)**. Positioning the second requires some care. One method could be to employ a height gage, but I settled for measuring 25mm along the face from its lower (non-chamfered) edge. Eagle-eyed readers may note that when the tool holder locations were later drilled in the turret, they did not fall perfectly midway along the conical face, probably indicating an error of a few thousandths in setting this point on the body.

This hole was drilled 8.5mm then tapped M10 for the pivot **(Photo 10.12)**. Surplus material can then sawn away using the slitting saw **(Photo 10.13)**, after which two holes may be drilled one for the detent spring, the other for its 2.0mm pivot rod

10.15 *Slitting saw used to cut slot for detent*

(Photo 10.14). As regards the spring, I found one which measured 3.7mm diameter and about 13mm long. The hole was drilled 4mm diameter, and some 13mm deep. The spring would thus be compressed reasonably when all was later assembled.

The slitting saw was then used to cut the slot which will house the detent **(Photo 10.15)**. **Photo 10.16** shows the thinned gage plate being checked for size in the slot.

ARBOR

The price of blank arbors has become very reasonable in recent years. Alternatively, you can penny pinch like me and make one. The raw material was a length of 19mm diameter En 1a (similar to 12L14) free machining bar. As this could be passed through the headstock of the Chipmaster without cutting to length, I chose this machine, which also offered greater topslide travel.

10.16 *Gage plate has been thinned to fit slot*

10.17 *Method of setting topslide to cut Morse taper*

The procedure for setting over the top slide to the required half angle was as follows. A small piece of scrap bar was gripped in the chuck, then faced and centered. A number two Morse taper center was then gripped between this female center and the tailstock. A clock gage was then fitted to the toolpost and the topslide angle adjusted until the slide could be moved, taking the clock along the length of the taper with no movement of the reading. The saddle had previously been moved to a suitable position and locked. **Photo 10.17** shows the setup for this.

The taper was then produced, taking successive cuts by feeding along on the topslide. The Zeus book gives the small end diameter as 0.572in. (14.53mm) so I aimed to be just a thousandth or two larger. As you approach the final size, the accuracy of the taper may be checked by using a MT2-3 adapter sleeve. If the sleeve is fitted with just a gentle push, you may then be able to detect slight radial movement at one end. In my case, it was at the small end farther from the chuck, so a bit of finishing work with a smooth file on the opposite end was in order to shave away a little material.

Once the fit was obtained with no discernible movement, the arbor end was drilled and tapped M10 to take either a draw bar or dummy tang for ejection. **Photo 10.18** shows the work just prior to parting off.

The work was then located in the headstock taper of the Myford and the end machined to give a close fit in the corresponding bore in the body **(Photo 10.19)**. Once this was achieved, a small flat was filed along the diameter. This would allow air to escape when assembling with Loctite.

DETENT (FIG 10.4)

I made mine from a piece of ⅟₁₆in. gage plate found in the scrap box. The problem that then arose was that this material would not slide into the slot cut with a nominal ¹⁄₁₆in. slitting saw. I therefore suggest that other prospective builders cut the slot with a ¹⁄₁₆in. thick slitting saw, but use 1.5mm material for the detent, which should give just a little clearance. My solution was to take a thousandth or two off the thickness using a surface grinder. The work was drilled then sawn and filed to the shape required, which was determined after trial assembly.

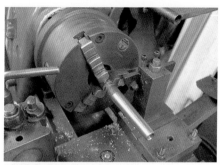

10.18 *Parting off the arbor*

ASSEMBLY

The arbor should now be Loctited to the body and given time to cure. The detent with spring and pin should also be added, along with the turret and pivot.

DRILLING TOOL LOCATIONS

The assembly is now fitted to the lathe tailstock, ensuring that the detent is correctly located in a turret slot. Using a center drill held in the chuck **(Photo 10.20)**, the first tool location is started by advancing the tailstock into the drill. This is repeated for the other four positions. A 9mm drill is then substituted for the center drill, and the five holes drilled to a depth of 18mm. Finally the process is repeated with a 10mm drill to give close fitting 10mm diameter sockets **(Photo 10.21)**.

Even if slight errors exist in the positions of the turret slots, because they are drilled on the machine, each of the five tool sockets will be accurately positioned on center when selected for engagement.

CLAMP SCREWS

The work was taken back to the mill, where it was gripped in the vise with the lower face of the body horizontal. With the detent engaged in a turret slot, the table was adjusted in the Y axis to bring a drill central

10.19 *Arbor held in the Myford headstock to machine body location diameter*

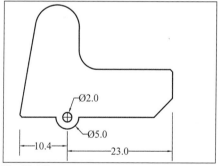

Fig 10.4 *Detent*

Ø2.0
Ø5.0
10.4
23.0

10.20 *Embryo turret is fed into center drill to start tool locations*

10.21 *A 10mm drill is employed to give the finished size*

10.22 *Starting work on the clamp screw holes*

10.23 *Tapping is finished by hand*

to the lower socket, then in the X direction to set the position along the axis of the socket. My "Heineken" center drill ("reaches the parts…") was then used to start each of the five holes **(Photo 10.22)** which were then drilled 3.3mm and tapped M4. Tapping was started under power to ensure squareness, then finished by hand **(Photo 10.23)**.

The turret, detent etc. were then dismantled, cleaned of swarf, and reassembled **(Photo 10.24)**. The pin had been reduced in length, and the two ends of its location hole lightly peened over for retention.

TOOL HOLDERS

These are simple items, turned to fit the sockets, then drilled to take the chosen tool, typically center drill or drill. They may be made solid, in which case the tool will be retained by a setscrew or Loctite. Alternatively, for tools of about 6mm diameter and above, the holder may be split lengthwise, in which case the turret clamp screw will serve the dual purpose of locking both the holder and the tool. In either case a flat should be filed for the screw to engage upon. Without this, there is the possibility that the clamp screw will raise a burr which could make it difficult to remove

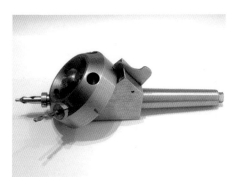

10.24 *Completed turret device*

the holder. It is also possible to make small
D-bits to fit directly in the sockets.

OPERATION

To ensure tool clearance, it may be necessary
to shorten standard jobber drills, or purchase
stub drills. Fitted to my Super Seven, I found
that the tooling illustrated just cleared the
two toolposts. The rear post is the standard
Myford issue, but fitted with an adapter
block to move the part off tool closer to the
chuck. The front is my home-brewed version
of a quick change type. The commercially
available quick change toolpost is somewhat
smaller than my home-brewed variety and
should give a bit more room to play with.

CHAPTER 11
DIVIDING HEAD - SIMPLE

In the *Mini-Lathe* book, Chapter 5 included a headstock dividing attachment, which could be used to index work held in the spindle chuck. This, in turn, was employed to create the divisions on handwheels and could be used in conjunction with the guided center punch or powered toolpost spindle. However, if we are to perform dividing functions on separately held work, using the headstock spindle as the tool driver, then a different approach is required.

My first thought was to look at the dividing head designs published in Model Engineers' Workshop by Harold Hall. However, these lend themselves more to applications where there is a milling machine table for mounting. The concept examined was one familiar to model engineers for the last fifty years or so, in the beautifully executed dividing head made by Myford for use with the Seven series lathes. It is also noted that Hemingway kits have resurrected a conceptually similar device designed by Westbury, and marketed by them as kit number HK2130.

As the Mini-Lathe is considerable lighter than a Myford, the primary aim was to produce something smaller, and the secondary aim to employ stock materials, thus avoiding the complexity of pattern making and the cost of castings. One of the first decisions to be made

concerned the manner of work holding. Given that parts made on these lathes are likely to be small, an ER 20 collet nose was selected, as this series would allow work of up to 13mm diameter to be gripped.

This dividing device can be made in two ways: the simple way described in this chapter, where direct division is accomplished by a plunger acting on suitable lathe change wheels, or the more complex version covered in Chapter 12, where a wormwheel and division plates are added.

On the metric machine, the supplied wheels include 30, 35, 40, 50, 60, and 80 teeth. Thus divisions of 3, 4, 5, 6, 7, 8, 10, 12, 15, 20, 25, 30, 35, 40, 50, 60, and 80 will be directly available. The imperial version of the lathe comes with wheels having tooth numbers which include 30, 35, 40, 45, 50, 55, 57, 60 and 65. Thus the additional factors of 9, 11, and 19 become possible.

In both of these cases, the figures above result when using a "single point" plunger which engages in the valley between two teeth. If a "split point" plunger is fitted, as advocated by Harold Hall, then it becomes possible to double up on each of the division factors. (The plunger point is designed with a tooth shaped cutout, so that when rotated 90 degrees, it locates over one tooth instead of between two. Should owners of either metric or imperial machines require additional change wheels, then these are readily available at modest cost.

The initial intention was to mount the head directly in place of the topslide. However, once tried, it was clear that there would be a benefit in allowing the assembly to move toward the operator. This gave rise to the baseplate-pillar combination now proposed.

Two main mounting arrangements are offered. The first locates the dividing head in place of the topslide and sets its axis at lathe center height. The second makes use of the vertical slide with or without the milling sub table described in *MEW* Issue 136. This would allow the axis to be raised, lowered and inclined in two planes, allowing operations such as gear cutting.

MANUFACTURE

Because one or two of the parts are quite chunky, I recommend you use larger machinery if it is available, through your model engineering society or technical college. Nevertheless, I believe that the various components can be produced on a Mini-Lathe, and have included photos of some setups to illustrate. However, while time may not be money, it is increasingly precious, and so I have used the heavier equipment available to speed up proceedings. The Mini-Lathe was also kept clear of work to permit frequent checks on fitting the dividing head to the machine as work progressed.

MAIN BODY (FIG 11.1)

My initial inclination was to use a slab of aluminum, as it is easier to machine and, while less rigid than steel, would be quite satisfactory here. Unfortunately, the piece available was just not large enough. The material I then chose was a length of mild

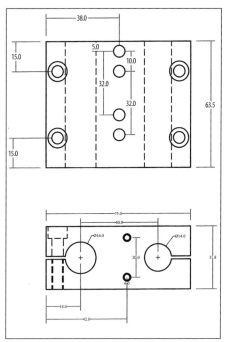

Fig 11.1 *Body. Notes – drill and ream 16mm and 14mm dia holes. Four locations for clamp bolts are tapped through, drilled 6 dia to slot and counterbored 10 dia x 6 deep. Some hidden detail omitted*

steel flat bar 2.5in. x 1.25in. (63.5mm x 31.75mm) cut and squared off to a length of 75mm. The most important aspects of this part are the two bores which will house the spindle and the steady arm. Care should be taken to ensure that they are parallel, at the correct spacing and held close to size. Ironically, the size question is more important for the steady arm, which is made from stock material. If the bore for the spindle comes in on the large size, then simply turn the spindle location diameter to suit.

Two sets of holes have been shown for the location bolts (M6 threaded rod) The first set was drilled roughly central for appearance,

11.01 *Body material held in four jaw chuck for facing*

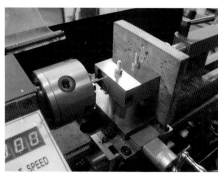

11.02 *Work held on the saddle, pressure applied from the tailstock*

11.03 *Drilling the body*

11.04 *Reaming the bore for the spindle*

then after roughly setting in position on the Mini-Lathe I decided to add a second set to allow the assembly to be moved farther from the centerline. A later addition was the base plate, which allowed considerably greater movement.

Photo 11.01 shows that it is possible to hold this chunk of metal in the four jaw chuck, and **Photo 11.02** (the material has now been scrubbed up) illustrates a setup for drilling the two major holes, pressure being applied via a block of wood from the tailstock. However, I opted to deal with these operations on the mill,

drilling as in **Photo 11.03** followed by reaming **(Photo 11.04)**.

The positions for the four clamp bolts were drilled through tapping size (5mm) then counterbored 10mm diameter to a depth of 6mm to accommodate the heads of the M6 socket head capscrews.

The two slots were then cut with a slitting saw **(Photo 11.05)**. Following this, the holes were opened out to 6mm down to the slot. It would probably be more efficient to do the opening out at the earlier setting, but it needs reasonably careful attention to the depth. By

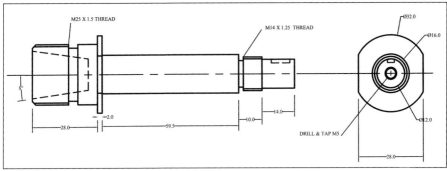

Fig 11.2 *Spindle*

drilling down to the slot it is easy to feel when the correct depth is achieved.

Two drilled and tapped holes are required to locate the plunger support pillar. It will depend on the equipment and methods available to you whether these are covered at this stage or more easily spotted through after the mating part is made.

SPINDLE (FIG 2)

As noted, I chose to adopt the ER 20 fitting for workholding, and accordingly purchased a 10mm collet and a commercial closing nut. The nuts can be obtained quite cheaply, come with the internal extraction ring, and are hardened. It is really not worth the bother of making one.

Working with a length of 32mm free-cutting steel bar as a first stage, I machined the features for the collet housing (8-degree half angle), taking this out so that the extraction groove of the uncompressed collet stood out from the housing by about 4mm **(Photo 11.06)**. Trigonometry showed that this should be about the right allowance for the 1mm collapse on diameter. This was followed by cutting the M25 x 1.5 thread to match the purchased nut.

Purists would probably prefer to finish turn between centers. However, having established

11.05 *Slitting saw used to cut slots*

11.06 *Collet is tried for size, about 4mm projection to the extraction groove*

11.07 *The nut was checked for true running*

11.08 – *but was still gripped in the four jaw and the work clocked.*

11.09 *Cutting the 3mm keyway in the spindle*

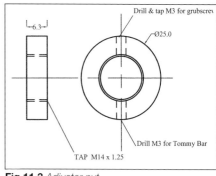

Fig 11.3 *Adjuster nut*

(**Photo 11.07**) that the outer diameter of the nut (tightened with a 10mm drill in the collet) showed negligible deviation on the DTI, I reckoned that if the work was centered using the Colchester collet, then the overall accuracy would be more than acceptable. **Photo 11.08** shows the start of work on the main length of the spindle. The nut has been gripped and accurately centered in the four jaw. After dealing with the remaining turned features, the work was transferred to the mill (**Photo 11.09**) to cut the 3mm keyway.

ADJUSTER NUT (FIG 11.3)

A short length of steel bar (25mm diameter) was bored 12.8mm diameter, then parted off (**Photo 11.10**) and faced to a thickness

11.10 *Parting off the embryo adjuster nut*

of about 6.3mm. It was then nipped in the chuck, squared up, gripped firmly and tapped M14 x 1.25. This gave a reasonably fine

11.11 *Commencing the part off operation on the spacer*

thread for adjustment purposes. The work was then taken to the mill to add the holes for setscrew and tommy bar.

SPACER AND WASHER (FIG 11.4)

A spacer is fitted which abuts the adjuster nut, covers the end of the thread and provides a reasonable area of face in contact with the division gear. I used 22mm diameter bar and it is a simple matter of turning, facing, drilling through, counterboring and parting off **(Photo 11.11)**. A thick washer cut from 16mm bar, is placed under the countersunk gear retaining screw.

STEADY BRACKET (FIG 11.5)

A piece of 20mm x 30mm mild steel was sawn to a length of 66mm, then drilled 14mm and drilled and tapped M8. Here it is important to have these two features parallel and spaced accurately to match the bore spacing in the body. As with the body, the work is slotted, using a 1.5mm slitting saw, then drilled, tapped and counterbored for the M6 clamp screw. The completed part is shown in Photo **11.12**.

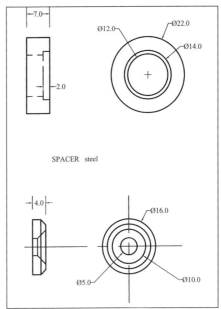

Fig 11.4 *Spacer and washer*

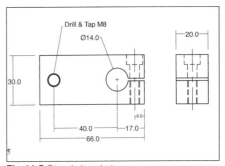

Fig 11.5 *Steady bracket*

11.12 *The finished steady bracket*

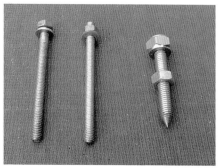

11.13 *Adjuster screw on right shown with the two threaded rods*

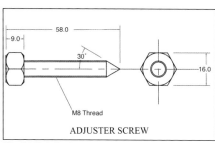

Fig 11.6 *Adjuster screw*

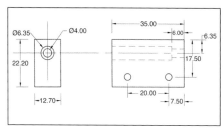

Fig 11.7 *Plunger body*

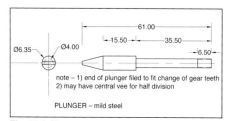

Fig 11.8 *Plunger*

ADJUSTER SCREW (FIG 11.6)

This part is intended to screw into the steady bracket and give a form of "tailstock" support to long slender items. Mine was made in the simplest possible manner by using a length of M8 mild steel threaded rod, turning one end to a 60-degree point, then Loctiting on a knob turned from a piece of 16mm hex brass with a matching tapped hole. The completed part is shown in **Photo 11.13** alongside two 80mm lengths of M6 threaded rod used to hold the dividing head down to the saddle.

PLUNGER SUB-ASSEMBLY (FIGS 11.7, 11.8, AND 11.9)

The three parts here are those used for the headstock dividing attachment described in Chapter 5 of the *Mini-Lathe* book. Accordingly, the drawings are reproduced here, but the description is not repeated. The spring used was as follows: OD 5.5mm, wire diameter 0.6mm, free length 32mm, compressed (coil bound) length 12mm. The plunger arrangement may be seen in **Photo 11.14** which shows the head assembly off the machine.

PLUNGER SUPPORT PILLAR (FIG 11.10)

A piece of 16mm x 8mm aluminum flat was cut to a length of 101mm. It then requires a total of eight holes. Two are drilled and countersunk to take the attachment screws, and it may be that you use these to position the mating tapped holes in the body. Six further holes are indicated, these being drilled and tapped M3 to give three positions for the plunger assembly so that it can engage with different sizes of gear.

The positions give are those measured after construction, but the manner of their location was simply to fit different gears, place the plunger where it looked right, and mark through. The part may be seen in position in **Photo 11.14**.

SPACER PLATE (FIG 11.11)

This part functions simply to bring the plunger detent roughly to the center of the gear teeth, and was made from a small piece of aluminum flat, 5mm thick. The thickness does not need to be exact. Check on the job, but I expect anything between about 4mm and 6.35mm would suffice. The important points are the two holes drilled at 20mm spacing. Again, if your pitching is not accurate then just open up the holes a few thousandths. It may also be seen between the support pillar and the plunger body in **Photo 11.14**.

STEADY ARM

This part is not drawn, being a piece of 14mm cold-rolled bar cut and faced to my

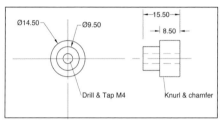

Fig 11.9 *Plunger knob*

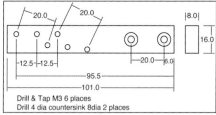

Fig 11.10 *Plunger support pillar*

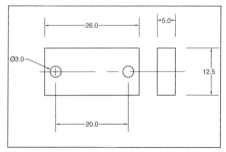

Fig 11.11 *Spacer plate*

11.14 *Head assembly fitted with forty tooth gear*

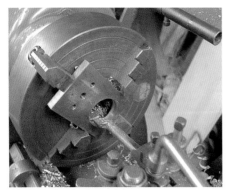

11.15 *Boring the baseplate*

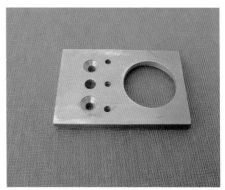

11.16 *Completed baseplate*

chosen length of 250mm. Others may choose to go shorter or longer depending on the applications envisaged.

BASE PLATE (FIG 11.12)

A length of cold-rolled flat steel 63.5mm x 9.5mm was cut to a length of 96mm. The two countersunk holes are designed to accommodate M6 screws which attach the assembly to the existing topslide mounting in the saddle, while the three 5mm holes match those in the milling sub table. These features are all straightforward work.

It is also bored 40mm and counterbored 46mm using the four jaw in the lathe **(Photo 11.15)** to accept the clamp disk. Great accuracy is not needed, but care should be taken that the disk is then made to fit. The completed plate is shown in **Photo 11.16.**

CLAMP DISK (FIG 11.13)

If the clamping action is to function correctly, then care does need to be taken. When fitted, both of its surfaces should lie under flush with reference to the base plate. Thus, the overall thickness is given as 9.2mm and the spigot

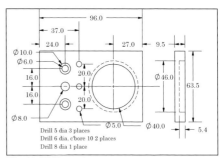

Fig 11.12 *Base plate*

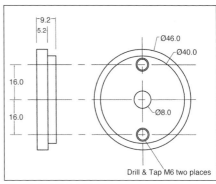

Fig 11.13 *Clamp disk*

depth as 4mm (compared with 9.5mm and 4.1mm on the plate).

To make the part, a slice of 2in. diameter free-cutting steel bar was turned down and faced. Taking the shoulder line slightly off center gave a little extra meat for the chuck to grip. The fit and depth were checked against the plate. While in the lathe, the central 8mm hole was also drilled. The part was then taken to the mill, where the 8mm hole was used as a datum to set the positions for the two M6 tapped holes.

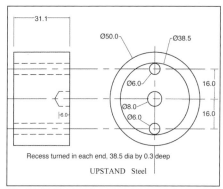

Fig 11.14 *Upstand*

UPSTAND (FIG 11.14)

As noted previously, the original intention was that this should be the sole means of support on the saddle, but a rethink introduced the baseplate. If you choose to follow my suggestion here, then the axial length of the upstand is set so that when assembled on the saddle, the axis of the dividing head is level with the lathe center height. This can be achieved either by careful measurement of the parts and the lathe, or as in my case (because I had already made the part before the baseplate was considered) by making it slightly long, assembling on the machine, and taking height measurements to 10mm tools held in the dividing head and in the tailstock.

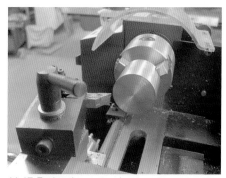

11.17 *Facing the upstand*

As is shown on the drawing, the correct size for my setup was 31.1mm, but do check on the job. You may also consider an alternative approach by making the baseplate, clamp disk and upstand first, then positioning the bores in the body, after trial assembly.

Making the part was a case of using the lathe to clean up a piece of bar **(Photo 11.17)** then deal with the other turned features, before transferring to the mill and using the same datum method as on the

11.18 *8mm rod is used to find the datum*

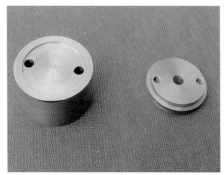

11.19 *Completed upstand (left) and clamp disk (right)*

clamp disk **(Photo 11.18)** to add the 6mm holes. Shallow recesses are specified at both ends to ensure that, when clamped up, the parts locate squarely. **Photo 11.19** illustrates the completed upstand and clamp disk.

OPERATION

The final three photos endeavour to show ways in which the dividing head may be rigged on the Mini-Lathe. In **Photo 11.20**, the base plate is bolted down in place of the topslide, using two countersunk M6 Allen screws of 19mm overall length.

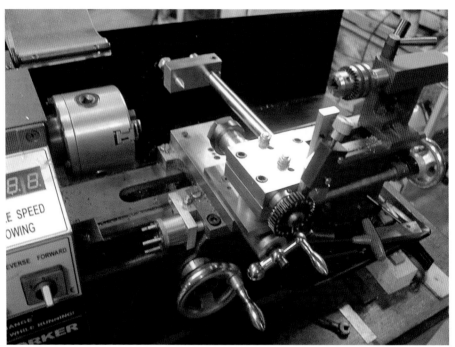

11.20 *Here the head is bolted down to the saddle in place of the topslide. Although shown at right angles to the machine bed it may be rotated about a vertical axis. The head axis is at lathe center height.*

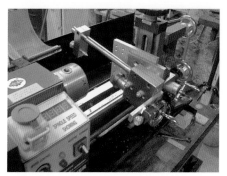

11.21 *In this view, the head is attached to the milling sub plate and in turn to the vertical slide.*

In this arrangement, the head centerline is automatically at lathe center height, and the head may be rotated on two vertical axes, that of the absent topslide, and the centerline of the upstand.

The vertical slide and milling sub table are employed in **Photo 11.21**, where the head is again held by the base plate, this time bolted to the sub table by three M5 screws. **Photo 11.22** shows a simpler arrangement where the body of the dividing head is located directly in the vertical slide, packing being added to protect the surface. Note, however, that in this setup, the steady arm should be fitted to ensure rigid clamping. Here the head may be rotated on the horizontal and vertical axes afforded by the vertical slide, with a third (horizontal) axis (upstand) being available in **Photo 11.21**.

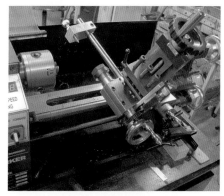

11.22 *The head is now clamped (with protective packing) by the vise on the vertical slide. This arrangement and that in Photo 11.21 permit rotation about both horizontal and vertical axes.*

CHAPTER 12

DIVIDING HEAD WITH WORM

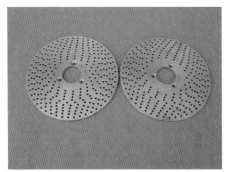

12.01 *Two division plates made by spotting through from masters*

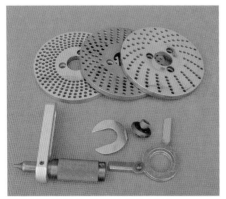

12.02 *Kit of parts, division plates and associated parts available from Warco and other suppliers*

The previous chapter covered dividing by use of a plunger acting on a selected changewheel to give the required divisions. We now examine the possibility of adding a worm drive, division plate(s), and sector arms typical of a workshop dividing head. In the case of the Myford item, these features are standard, while for the Hemingway, a supplementary kit of parts is available to add the facility.

Many years ago, I produced the pair of division plates shown in **Photo 12.01**, these being made by spotting through from a pair owned by a friend. My initial inclination was to put these to good use, and indeed to turn a suitable worm. The Mini-Lathe change wheels have a One Mod tooth form, so that the matching worm would have a pitch of a little over 3mm, and turning this would take some time and care on the small machine. I decided therefore to also look at commercial sources, and found that HPC Gears supply a correctly sized budget worm at modest cost (although the postage costs about the same again). This gear (Ref EW1-1) was selected as being suitable.

My attention then turned to the division plates, and looking at the Warco website I

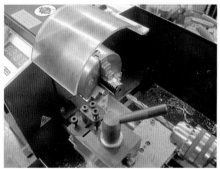

12.03 *Worm bore is opened up to 8mm by drilling and reaming. Note protection from chuck jaws*

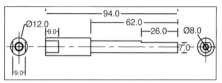

Fig 12.1 *Spindle*

12.04 *End of spindle is tapped M4*

found that a set of three plates with sector arms and handle with plunger are offered as an add-on set for the Vertex HV6 rotary table. These parts are the same as those fitted to the BS-0 dividing head from the same manufacturer, so to illustrate the build, I have borrowed the relevant components from my Vertex dividing head **(Photo 12.02)**.

The price shown on the Warco website at time of writing was around $45 for the add-on set, which got me thinking about the work involved in making the parts (there are some 525 division holes, as well as the general turning, milling etc. My own assessment was that buying in this kit really was a no brainer, but for any who do wish to make their own plates, then they may then be made by working from the method advocated by Maurice Turnbull *(Model Engineer,* 31st August 2007)*, i.e. draw in CAD, print, stick paper on metal, and spot through. There may well be slight positional errors, but the effect will be reduced by the 1 to 40 worm/ wheel ratio.

Once I had made the decision to source these parts commercially, the exercise was reduced essentially to making a shaft, housings and bracket.

WORM

This was modified by opening up the bore by drilling **(Photo 12.03)** and reaming to 8mm. It comes with a 4mm setscrew, and this is used to engage on a flat on the spindle allowing axial movement for endfloat adjustment.

SPINDLE (FIG 12.1)

I cut a length of free-machining bar 12mm diameter, faced to 94mm length and centered at each end. It was then turned down to 8mm diameter for a length of 62mm, this diameter being checked for a good sliding fit in the

12.05 *Two flats are milled for handle –*

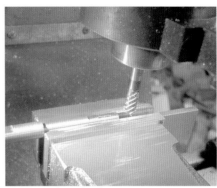

12.06 *– and one for the worm setscrew.*

worm. The two ends were then tapped M4 **(Photo 12.04)** and M6.

On the milling machine, two flats were cut at the 12mm diameter end **(Photo 12.05)** to accept the Vertex handle and one on the 8mm diameter **(Photo 12.06)** for the worm setscrew. These jobs could equally have been undertaken on the Mini-Lathe using a filing rest and headstock dividing attachment.

SPACER (FIG 12.2)

This part, shown being drilled in **Photo 12.07**, functions simply to set the handle out at the correct axial distance from the division plate. The measurements given are for the part as made. As the handle plunger has several millimeters of effective travel, it is likely that a fair amount of leeway exists here as regards the thickness. Nevertheless, I suggest checking on the job at assembly, and being prepared to adjust as necessary.

PLATE SUPPORT (FIG 12.3)

I chose to make this in two parts, Loctited together, in an effort to reduce swarf generation, although it may well have been counterproductive in terms of time. You

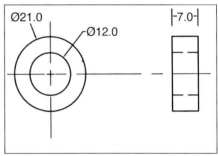

Ø21.0   Ø12.0 |–7.0–|

Fig 12.2 *Spacer*

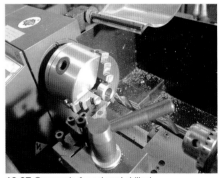

12.07 *Spacer is faced and drilled*

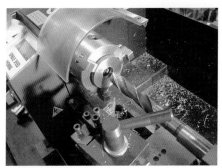

12.08 *For the two part assembly, the disk is drilled 19mm*

12.09 *Second part has groove cut*

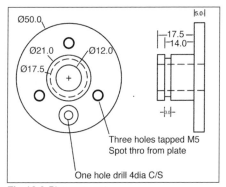

Fig 12.3 *Plate support*

12.10 *Spotting through for plate attachment*

could equally well turn the part from one lump of 50mm or 2 in. diameter steel bar. Free machining makes life a lot easier. **Photo 12.08** shows the disk being turned on the Mini-Lathe, while **Photo 12.09** shows the mating part after grooving. Here it was convenient to use the Myford, as the rear part off tool employed to cut the groove is always in position and ready for use.

One feature which does require a bit of care is the position of the groove which locates the spring clip, which in turn retains and applies a friction force to the sector arms. The drawings reflect the dimensions after some trial and error. Then one of the M5 holes was spotted through from one of the division plates, then tapped **(Photo 12.10)**. With a screw in place to hold the plate, the process is repeated for the other two positions. The 4mm hole is then drilled and countersunk so that the head will be underflush and clear the underside of the division plate.

BODY (FIG 12.4)

A piece of 30mm x 20mm rectangular section steel bar was cut to a length of about 45mm and faced at one end **(Photo 12.11)**. As the design was proceeding to some extent "on the hoof," this seemed a suitable length,

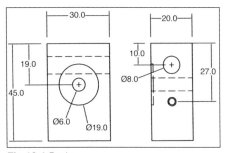

Fig 12.4 *Body*

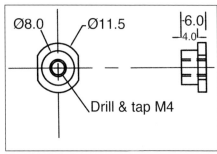

Fig 12.5 *Spindle nut*

12.11 *Preparing to face the body*

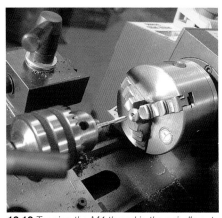

12.12 *Tapping the M4 thread in the spindle nut*

although now completed, it looks as though 35mm would have been sufficient. Three holes are required: the first drilled and reamed to give a bearing for the spindle, the second drilled 6mm for the attachment threaded rod, and the third drilled and tapped to accept the screw which will retain the plate support.

The first two are dealt with initially, then the spindle is used to align the plate support, so that the position of the M4 hole may be spotted through, then drilled and tapped. A feature added as an afterthought is the counterbore/relief around the 6mm hole, cut

out to about 19mm diameter and 0.2mm deep. This is merely to shift the frictional contact area outwards when clamped up, ensuring a firm assembly.

SPINDLE NUT (FIG 12.5)

This part is something of an embellishment, as an ordinary M4 nut and plain washer would function just as well. However, I do feel that it adds a little to the appearance. A piece of 12mm free-machining steel was cleaned to about 11.5mm then the 8mm spigot turned to fit the worm. Axial lengths are not at all critical. After parting off, it was drilled through

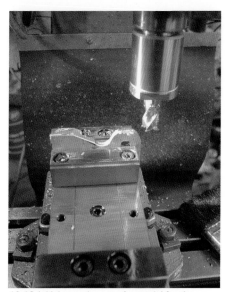

12.13 *Initial squaring up of material for the bracket.*

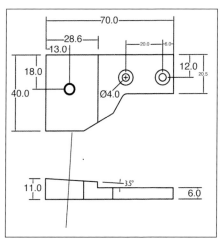

Fig 12.6 *Bracket*

3.3mm and tapped M4. **Photo 12.12** shows the tapping operation. Finally a couple of flats were filed to take a 10mm wrench.

BRACKET (FIG 12.6)

There are probably two schools of thought regarding meshing the worm with a straight cut change wheel. In an ideal situation, the worm would mesh with a purpose-made worm wheel having curved teeth with extensive lines of contact. The next best, frequently employed, approach is to use a wheel with helically cut teeth, which then also allows the shafts to be set at right angles.

Here, while the pitch of the worm (1 Mod) should match that of the wheel when set at right angles, if the shafts are set this way, then "cape and corner" tooth contact results. If the worm and a changewheel are manually held together, they happily assume the angle of the worm, about three and a half degrees. (HPC quote the helix angle of the worm as three degrees 25min.) I therefore took the decision to set the wormshaft over at about this angle, and the design of the bracket reflects this.

The bracket material turned out to be another instance of recycling. About ten years ago, a lever arm had been milled to shape, as part of an exercise to build a remote operator unit for an item of 11000-volt switchgear. A section of the prototype arm was sawn off and squared up in the mill **(Photo 12.13)**. After further trimming, the two location holes were drilled then the end squared back to be flush when assembled **(Photo 12.14)**. To achieve a fair approximation to the three and a half degrees, an $^{11}/_{64}$in. (4.4mm) drill was used as packing under one end. The work was gripped in the vise **(Photo 12.15)** and the

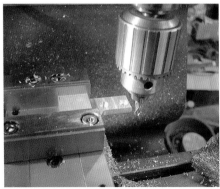

12.14 *End of bracket is trimmed to be flush with main head body*

12.15 *End of bracket was raised with drill to give approx correct slope*

inclined face cut with an end mill. It may be noted that here the mill vise has been changed for the Warco DH-1. The Warco WM-18 mill has now been returned to Warco following its review in *MEW* Issue 153, but, for the present, I have been able to hang on to the Doug House-designed vise, and have been putting it to good use.

SUNDRY ITEMS – THREADED ROD

Two lengths of threaded rod are needed: one piece of M6 cut to around 42mm in length, and one of M4 cut to about 28mm. Also required are M4 x 12 countersunk Allen screws plus nut, and an M6 nut and washer.

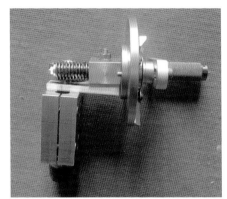

12.16 *This view shows the inclination and effect on gear mesh.*

12.17 *View on underside showing component parts*

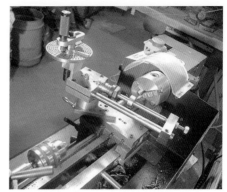

12.18 *Dividing head set up on Mini-Lathe to drill into a conical surface.*

ASSEMBLY AND OPERATION

Photos 12.16 and 12.17 show two views of the worm system attached to the head described in the earlier article. The plate and sector arm are fitted, followed by the handle and plunger. The worm is then added to the spindle, endfloat being adjusted by the spindle nut and M4 locknut. The worm setscrew is then tightened on to the flat.

The body is fitted to the bracket, the worm held in contact with the changewheel and the retaining nut tightened. Pivoting the body on the threaded rod allows the meshing to be adjusted to eliminate backlash. **Photo 12.18** shows the completed unit fitted to the Mini-Lathe in one of the possible setups, this one to drill holes in a tapered workpiece.

CHAPTER 13
PUMP CENTER

I first came across this concept in an article by Peter Rawlinson published in *Model Engineers' Workshop* Issue 88, where the accessory was designed primarily as a tapping aid for use in medium-sized lathes, incorporating a No 3 Morse taper arbor, though the point was made that it could be reduced to No.2 to fit a typical model engineering lathe. I later came across a reference to a similar device in *Machine Shop Practice,* by K.H. Moltrecht, but here, the primary use was for centering up work in a four jaw chuck. My later Mark 2 version of the device is described below, and is seen used as a tapping aid in **Photo 13.01.**

Immediately after reading the *MEW* article, I latched on to the potential advantages of the gadget and decided to cobble up something similar. I use the term "cobble up" advisedly,

as it was probably put together in under half an hour, with the primary aim of assisting tapping in the mill. The parts of this are shown in **Photo 13.02** and it may be realized that no provision was made for keeping the components together. Thus, setting it up would require manual dexterity to keep every thing in its proper place. Nevertheless, the added convenience when tapping small threads has meant that the Heath Robinson version has survived, as made, for all of six years.

The primitive Mark 1 version was composed of just four parts: body, rear plug, spring, and rod. The body was a piece of ½in. (12.7mm) diameter by 16 gage steel tube, plugged at the rear with a press fit brass plug. A piece of ⅜in. (9.5mm) diameter bar

13.01 *The improved device used to guide a tap*

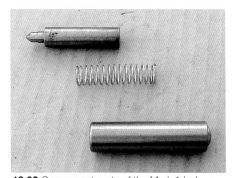

13.02 *Component parts of the Mark 1 lash up*

was given a point and pushed in after the spring.

More recently, when dealing with a small tapping job in the Mini-Lathe, it transpired that the standard tailstock chuck (10mm capacity) would not accept the original pump center. This provided the necessary impetus to make another, slightly smaller device, with means of retention for the rod and generally improved in terms of fit. The Mark 2 version has just five components, the extra one being a setscrew.

GENERAL DESIGN

I chose to use a ¼in. (6.35mm) diameter rod because 1) I had some suitable drill rod, and 2) because I also had a suitable reamer. If you work in metric, then by all means change to 6mm. As made, my version gives some 0.7in. (18mm) of compression movement, which is thought to be adequate for most model applications. The body, made from

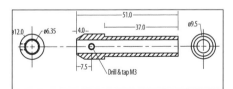

Fig 13.1 *Body*

13.03 *Turning down the location diameter for the body*

free-cutting mild steel bar is reduced for most of its length to under 10mm for easy accommodation in the chuck. A short section is left at the original (12mm) diameter allowing extra meat to take a setscrew. The sliding drill rod is given a 60-degree point at one end. A filed flatted section, working with the setscrew, restricts its travel.

In general, no great precision is needed to make this device, especially if it is to be used as a tapping aid. My original version has a decidedly sloppy fit but nevertheless gives good support for tapping. If, on the other hand, you plan to use it for centering work in a four jaw chuck, then a good sliding fit becomes more important. The other dimensions, especially lengths, should be considered as guidance rather than absolute requirements.

MANUFACTURE BODY (FIG 13.1)

Cut a length of 12mm diameter CRS bar and face to about 51mm. Grip in the three jaw with about 38mm showing, and turn down a length of 37mm to a diameter of 9.5mm **(Photo 13.03)**. Center drill and drill through ¹⁵⁄₆₄in. or 6mm, then ream ¼in. (6.35mm) If you do not have a suitable reamer, then open up by running a ¼in. drill through, taking care to feed slowly.

Reverse the work in the chuck, swing the topslide to 30 degrees and cut a generous chamfer for appearance **(Photo 13.04)**. If your bar is not in pristine condition, feel free to take a light cut to clean up the 12mm O.D.

Now drill and tap the location for the setscrew. I chose M3 (because I had some M3 brass threaded rod) but 5 or 6 BA would work well. The hole was drilled 2.5mm dia. then tapped by hand. After this, you need to run the reamer back through to remove the burrs

13.04 *Adding a chamfer*

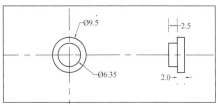

Fig 13.2 *Rear Cap*

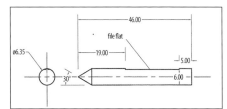

Fig 13.3 *Rod*

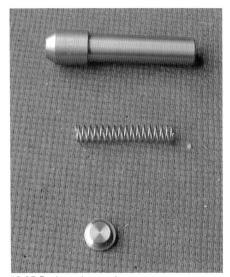

13.05 *Body, spring, and rear cap*

raised inside the bore. This is a good time to check the fit of the chosen drill rod.

REAR CAP (FIG 13.2)

The same 12mm free-cutting steel is used. Start by facing one end, then turn the shoulder to fit the ¼in. 6.35mm bore in the body. I chose to turn this with a slight interference, then file a slight taper. The

piece was then parted off and reversed to face and chamfer the other side. If you plan to use the finished article for centering, then drill a center while the work is on the lathe. I adopted a "belt and braces" approach to cap retention, adding a dab of Loctite 638 then pressing in. **Photo 13.05** shows the body, spring and cap.

ROD (FIG 13.3)

One essential feature of the rod is the flat into which the setscrew will engage. It can be a little tricky to hold things like this for filing, so I did this while there was still additional length to hold in the vise. The drill rod was first faced at one end. A quick dry assembly with the spring enabled the determination of the positions for the ends of the flat. It was then an easy matter to grip the rod in the vise **(Photo 13.06)** with this part in fresh air, and file down to achieve a thickness of about 6.0mm (i.e. about 0.35mm or 0.014in. metal removed). I then sawed the rod to length, after which it was gripped in the three jaw chuck, making sure that the jaws missed the flat. The topslide was then set over to create the 60-degree point, as shown in **Photo 13.07.**

SETSCREW

If you have a convenient screw, then by all means use it. I happened to have some offcuts of M3 brass threaded rod, so, taking one of these, I flattened one end by filing in the lathe and screwed it in to engage the flat. It was then sawn off about one millimeter clear of the body, filed slightly, then given a screwdriver slot courtesy of the jeweller's hacksaw. At this stage, it is worth checking the fit of the screw over the length of the flat and, if necessary, filing a little to achieve a level feature.

SPRING

I found a suitable spring among a bargain job lot. Its vital statistics are:

Coil diameter: 5.6mm
Wire diameter: 0.6mm
Free length: 31mm
Number of coils approx. 16

FINAL ASSEMBLY

This consisted of inserting the spring and rod into the body, then fitting the setscrew. It should be possible to nip the screw into place, then back off about a quarter of a turn and have a nice sliding fit of rod in body. If this is the case, then just add a smear of Loctite to keep the screw in place. **Photo 13.08** shows the comparison between the old and new versions.

13.06 *Work is easier to hold if left long*

13.07 *Top slide set over to machine the point*

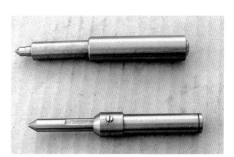

13.08 *Mark 1 above, improved Mark 2 below*

CHAPTER 14
SIMPLE DOUBLE ENDED TAILSTOCK DIEHOLDER

In the early 1990s, there was a short spell when work for the shop was thin on the ground, and I decided to look at the feasibility of producing tailstock die holders. The project got as far as a trial batch, machined principally on the manual Herbert 2D

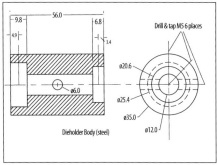

Fig 14.1 *Dieholder body*

14.01 *One set from the earlier batch, body has black oxide finish, bars are zinc plated*

capstan lathe, the thinking being that, if serious volume might be required, then the turning work could be assigned to either the automatic or manual machines.

The design was kept as simple as possible, the intention being that it would be mounted via a bar in the tailstock chuck, avoiding any need for Morse tapers. A set of three old parts is shown in **Photo 14.01**. The body is bored at one end to accept ¹³⁄₁₆in. and at the other, 1.000in. diameter dies, then being drilled through to match the mounting bar. It is also cross drilled to take a 6mm tommy bar. Although I was using industrial weight machinery at the time, the gadget can be easily made in an amateur setting. As an exercise here, I turned up a new, slightly shorter body, this time using the Mini-Lathe.

MANUFACTURE

The two minor components are really easy; just saw two pieces of bright steel bar, one 6mm diameter, the other 12mm, cut to roughly 80mm in length, then face and chamfer. Some pundits advocate a combined facing and chamfering tool, but now that quick change toolposts have become popular, I favor the use of a separate tool for each operation. If your normal tailstock chuck has a capacity of less than 12mm,

14.02 *Bandsaw takes the hard work out of sawing 35mm diameter*

14.03 *As a quick dodge to true up the work, it is pushed gently with the toolpost*

14.04 *Through hole is drilled in stages on a lightweight machine*

then reduce the diameter of one end of the mounting bar to allow it to be gripped.

The body starts life as 35mm diameter CRS bar, from which a piece about 56mm long is sawn **(Photo 14.02)**. Note that using the four jaw chuck would probably give a better grip, but I just fitted the alternate jaws for the three jaw. To get the work running true at its outer end, it was first nipped lightly and the lathe run at low speed. The toolpost was then gently backed into the work, gradually pushing it into a true running position **(Photo 14.03)**. The chuck was then tightened fully and the sequence of turning operations commenced. Here, it might have been better practice to fit a steady, however the facing work was undertaken with no problems using light cuts.

It was then centered and supported with a tailstock center. It could then be knurled using a straddle tool. The method adopted was to plunge feed across at the required position. This size of material is probably a bit much for this setup, and it shows in the quality of the knurled finish. Nevertheless, it does give a reasonably grippy surface. As the diameter at the ends was turned down slightly at a later stage, it might have been a better approach to turn down and then apply the knurling tool to a narrow width first before feeding axially to gain width.

Both ends of the job were treated in the same way, after which the drilling and boring was undertaken. The Mini-Lathe is, of course, not a powerful machine, so the hole was drilled in two stages, first with a 9.5mm drill then opening up with a 12mm **(Photo 14.04)**.

As noted previously (in paragraph two of this chapter), two sizes of die, ¹³⁄₁₆in. and 1.00in diameters would be accommodated. I believe that the nominal thicknesses for these die sizes are ¼in. and ⅜in. respectively. However, measuring a sample from

14.05 *Housings are bored to fit dies*

14.06 *Headstock dividing attachment fitted to Mini-Lathe*

the tool box, I found that for the smaller size the thickness ranged up to about 6.7mm, and for the larger up to 9.7mm. The drawings therefore show the housings to be slightly deeper than these figures. **Photo 14.05** shows one of these. In each case I allowed about 0.003in. (0.08mm) diametral clearance on nominal die size.

Virtually all of the dies in my collection are set and clamped in position using three screws spaced at intervals of 45 degrees. The outer two clamp, and the center locates in the split to control the thread diameter. To mark out the positions, the headstock dividing attachment was fitted **(Photo 14.06)** and horizontal lines scribed using a Vee tool on its side, as can be seen in **Photo 14.07**. To mark the axial positions, the Vee tool was set normally, and the work rotated against it by hand **(Photo 14.08)**. It then remained to drill and tap the holes to take the setscrews, and **Photo 14.09** shows the setup using the vertical slide.

As an afterthought, each end was lightly turned down as far as the start of the knurled band. This gave a slight improvement in appearance due to the sharply defined edge of the knurling.

14.07 *Angular positions scribed with Vee tool on side*

14.08 *Scribing axial positions*

14.09 *Drilling holes for setscrews*

14.10 *M6 thread cut on brass rod*

OPERATION

After fitting a complement of six setscrews (M5 x 8mm cone point), a thread was cut on a length of 6mm diameter brass rod **(Photo 14.10)**. At this sort of size, the holder may be hand held, while, for larger, the tommy bar might be required.

By no means are all dies are perfectly centered, and frequently tailstocks are not dead in line, so it is probably as well if the fit between body and mounting bar is slightly sloppy, so that the die may, within reason, find its own center.

Articles by Dyson Watkins appeared in *Model Engineers' Workshop* Issues 86 and 103, describing dieholder and toolholder designed specifically to float slightly and thus handle a modicum of misalignment.

CHAPTER 15
KNURLING

My interest in this subject was resurrected by the rekindling of enthusiasm for aero-modeling, with the associated need to make spare parts for one existing and, perhaps later, a new small engine. The first positive requirement was for a needle valve assembly for an old E.D. Racer diesel engine **(Photo 15.01)**, where a spring bearing against a straight knurled surface prevents mixture change under vibration. A second application which is expected to arise later will be in connection with a prop driver for a homemade motor, which would typically carry radial knurling to grip the rear face of the propeller.

15.01 *This E D Racer was acquired minus venturi and needle valve assembly*

Knurling is one of those topics that we tend to take for granted, although it can pose problems. In an industrial setting, when a high batch volume is the case, it's easy to do a few trial runs to optimize settings, notably depth, speed and feed. It is also easy to apply lots of cross slide pressure with a large capstan or CNC lathe. For the amateur, things are often somewhat different. First, we may be making just one part, and if the knurling operation is one of the last, then a failed process may imply a time-consuming remake. Second, our machines tend to be smaller and lighter, and generating large forces may not be the best way to achieve lathe longevity or continued precision.

The conventional process is generally thought of as one in which the metal is plastically deformed, as opposed to cut. My own feeling is that, while deformation is the principal action, this can over-simplify matters, as a certain amount of fine swarf is usually to be seen on the knurling rolls, implying that at least a small amount of metal has been released, either by cutting or rubbing. What is clear is that in conventional knurling, due to the deformation, the diameter of work grows quite a bit when knurled, and as a result, the process can be used either to salvage an undersize component or to create an increased outer diameter in preparation for press fitting.

Typically, the knurling tool is mounted with the axis of the roll, or rolls, set parallel to the lathe axis.

SINGLE ROLL TOOLING

Photo 15.02 shows a selection of tools each having a single knurl wheel. The photo should be self-explanatory; each is simply a piece of square bar, slotted and cross drilled to take a single knurl wheel on a (usually ¼in dia.) spindle. In operation, these are set up on the toolpost with the bar at 90 degrees to the lathe axis. The knurl is then positioned to overlap the job by say a couple of millimeters, then fed in using the cross slide. The depth of feed will be a matter of judgment to achieve a "full knurl" pattern. A frequent problem is the creation of a half-size pattern, which usually means that a bit more depth is needed. The saddle may then be moved toward the chuck, to give the amount of coverage required for the job. Because the knurling pressure must be applied directly by the cross slide leadscrew, on hobby-size lathes my preference is rather to use a straddle tool.

STRADDLE OR CLAMP TYPE TOOLING

Here the pressure is applied within the tool framework, with much lower forces being transmitted through the machine. **Photo 15.03** shows two such tools. That shown uppermost in the picture was rattled together many years ago to produce batches of knurled "file"-like devices for removing flash from moldings. As can be seen from the standard of finish and method of construction, it was built very much against the clock. Nevertheless, it did successfully produce many satisfactory parts over a period of several years, being worked initially on a Colchester Bantam, and later on a Chipmaster. The second tool shown has been used successfully on the Mini-Lathe and other machines.

As both of these tools are equipped with left- and right-hand spiral knurl wheels, the indentation produced is the typical diamond pattern. One of the applications envisaged was straight knurls on small diameter brass (needle valve assembly). Consequently, the

15.02 *Three homemade single wheel tools, two for straight and one for diamond patterns*

15.03 *Two straddle type tools: home-built welded lash above contrasts with the Arc Euro Trade version below*

next project was to make a straddle tool suitable for this sort of work.

Step one was to make a pair of hardened wheels. Many commercial wheels are about 19mm or even larger in diameter. My simplistic thinking leads me to believe that the crushing force will increase with both work diameter and wheel diameter, as the number of teeth in effective contact rises. It also seemed appropriate, as the work would be small, to use smaller wheels.

Conveniently, a length of ½in. diameter drill rod lay in the bits box just crying out to be liberated, and a quick exercise with calculator and CAD showed that at this size, 40 teeth would give a good approximation to a medium knurl. You can of course buy knurl wheels – they need not be expensive, but I was interested to try the DIY approach.

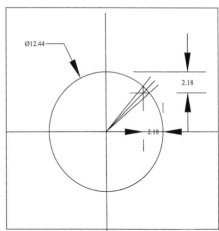

Sk 15.1 *Dimensional layout 40 teeth*

MAKING WHEELS

The bar was chucked and skimmed just sufficiently to clear any eccentricity. It was then drilled 5.5mm diameter to a depth of about 16mm. The work was transferred to the dividing head mounted on the mill with its axis accurately aligned with the table. A check was undertaken with a DTI to confirm that the work was indeed still running concentrically. An end mill was chosen which had sharp edges and sharp corners (round corners would translate to rounded knurling).

15.04 *Set up to cut forty straight teeth. A new cutter was selected to give sharp corners*

Using data gleaned from the CAD drawing **(Sk 15.1)**, the cutter was moved clear of the work, then positioned down from the top surface and fed in from the side by amounts (2.18mm) which would cut the groove at the 45-degree location. The table was fed along sufficiently to cut two wheels, with a part off allowance. The work was then moved back to clear the cutter, the dividing head handle advanced one complete turn, rotating the work nine degrees and the process repeated

to give forty teeth. **Photo 15.04** shows this operation in process.

The chuck, with the work, was returned to the lathe and the two wheels parted off. They were then hung on a wire, brought up to red heat using a blowlamp, held at temperature for a few minutes, then dunked in cold water. **Photo 15.05** shows them at this stage. A quick check with a file confirmed that they were now hard.

15.05 *The two wheels after roasting and dunking*

15.06 *A ⅟₁₆in. wide slitting saw was used to create the wheel slots*

BARS AND ARMS

The mounting bar and pressure arms are made from ½in. square mild steel bar, while the two vertical link bars are from half by quarter steel. **Figs 15.1, 15.2** and **15.3** give details of these.

The slots for the wheels were cut using a slitting saw **(Photo 15.06)**, while the recesses for the pressure pins were cut with a ⅜in. endmill **(Photo 15.07)**.

Construction of these various parts is quite straightforward, but note that the vertical links differ, in that for one the outer holes are drilled 6mm diameter, while the other has these positions tapped M5. In a similar manner, features on the upper and lower pressure arms are made specific to position, as can be seen from **Photo 15.08**. In general, no great accuracy is needed, but it is a good idea to make the wheels a neat fit in their slots with minimal side play.

15.07 *A ⅜in. end mill cuts a recess to match the pressure pin diameter*

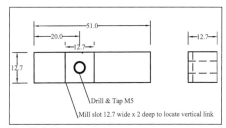

Fig 15.1 *Mounting bar*

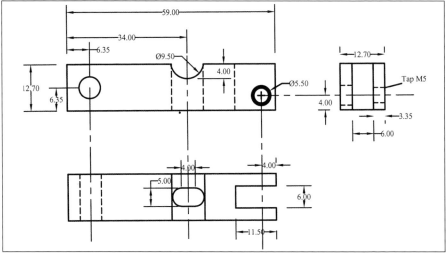

Fig 15.2 *Pressure arm*

15.08 *The completed top and bottom pressure arms*

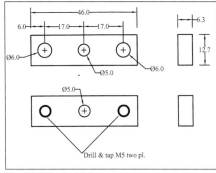

Fig 15.3 *Vertical links*

TURNED PARTS

To get the best from this tool, I recommend that some care be taken over the fit of these components. The spacer **(Fig 15.4)** should be just a couple of thousandths greater in length than the thickness of the pressure arms, and a similar comment applies to the length of the 6mm diameter sections on the two hex-headed shoulder bolts **(Fig 15.5)**. It also follows that these should fit closely in the drilled holes. Careful attention here will ensure that the assembled tool operates without sloppy sideways movement under load.

Note also that the wheel pivots **(Fig 15.6)** should be screwed in from the toolpost side, so that normal work rotation will tend to tighten them; also that the drawing does not show the screwdriver slots. Professionally made shoulder bolts would normally feature an undercut at the transition from shoulder to thread. In our small sizes, this seems to me

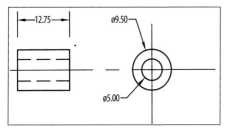

Fig 15.4 *Spacer*

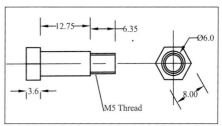

Fig 15.5 *Shoulder bolt*

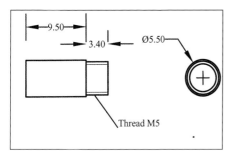

Fig 15.6 *Wheel pivot pin*

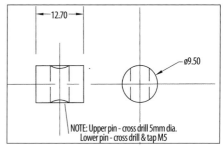

NOTE: Upper pin - cross drill 5mm dia.
Lower pin - cross drill & tap M5

Fig 15.8 *Pressure pin*

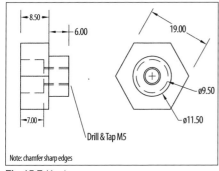

Note: chamfer sharp edges

Fig 15.7 *Knob*

to be a potential source of weakness, and so my preferred arrangement is to cut the thread normally, then to drill out a little of the female thread in the mating part, giving clearance. In my own example, as it will see relatively light use, I have used free-cutting mild steel (12L14) for these parts. For those intending more intensive applications, a change to a tougher or hardenable steel would most likely give longer life.

The Knob **(Fig 15.7)** was turned from a convenient off cut of ¾AF hex brass, tapped M5 to work on a length of M5 threaded rod to apply pressure. A saw cut was added later to give a visual indication for adjustment.

Two pressure pins **(Fig 15.8)** are needed to pass the compressive load into the arms. The upper is cross drilled 5mm dia. while the lower is drilled and tapped M5. A short length of M5 mild steel threaded rod acts as the adjustment screw and is retained by Loctite. Filing a small flat on the upper pin will give added contact area against the face of the knob.

OPERATION

In use, the wheels are adjusted down to contact the work and the saddle backed away to clear. The knob is then turned down to give the desired crush – this may be about half a turn. As with the single wheel tool, the saddle is then positioned to give about 2mm of overlap, then the wheels are fed into engagement by the cross slide. If a satisfactory pattern is not seen, start again with a different adjustment. Having achieved a satisfactory pattern, move the saddle as before to give the required length. Adding plenty of oil or coolant seems to help, and is probably beneficial in washing away fine debris.

The component parts of the tool can be seen in **Photo 15.09**, and the unit assembled in **Photo 15.10**.

RADIAL OR FACE KURLING

I mentioned at the beginning of this chapter that a second application would be to knurl the face of prop drivers for small model aero engines. **Photo 15.11** shows the factory-made driver on an ETA 29 engine from a similar bygone era to the ED Racer shown earlier. In the past, the approach adopted by some home enthusiasts has been to create this sort of pattern by cutting each line individually with a vee shaped tool, pushed in radially either by the cross slide or by a purpose made device similar to a keyway cutting or line engraving tool. This general approach will take a fair bit of time and careful indexing. I had formed the general impression that a tool to do this job would probably be similar in concept to a bevel gear, and this line of thinking was reinforced by some information found on the internet

15.09 *The components for the straddle tool*

15.10 *The assembled device viewed from the toolpost side*

15.11 *ETA 29 glow plug motor showing the knurled pattern on the prop driver*

via the excellent Ron Chernich web site: *www.modelenginenews.org*.

Again, the start was a bit of CAD drawing using an assumed prop driver diameter of 22mm and a maximum wheel diameter of about 12.0mm, i.e. again employing the trusty ½in. drill rod. **Sk 15.2** shows the general layout that resulted, the magic number for the taper being 33 degrees.

Making the wheel followed similar steps to those with the parallel wheels, the first step being to turn the conical form on the lathe. The chuck was again mounted on the dividing head. The tapered form introduced two added complications when cutting the teeth. First, if an endmill was used as before, at the 45-degree position, a spiral cut would result, so it was necessary to make a simple fly cutter with a 90-degree end, and to position this at work center height.

Second, as with bevel gears, the teeth should taper slightly, reducing in depth toward the center. From a bit more CAD work, I judged the cutting angle correction to be about one degree, and set the dividing head on the table at 34 degrees to take account of this. Again, forty teeth were cut, the setup being shown in **Photo 15.12**, and the hardened wheel in **Photo 15.13**. If this picture is examined carefully, a slight spiral effect can be detected, due to a slight error in cutter height.

Once again the mounting bar was made from ½in. square cold-rolled (although a bit rusty) steel stock, and here one end was first milled across at an angle of about 33 degrees, then drilled 0.25in. to accept a drill rod pivot pin, which was cut to length, tidied up and Loctited in place.

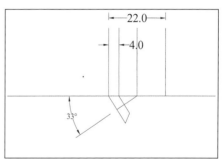

Sk 15.2 *Layout for face knurling*

15.12 *Setup for milling teeth on the conical wheel*

15.13 *Conical wheel now hardened*

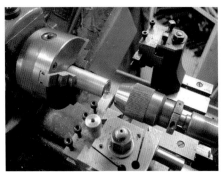

15.14 *My preferred setup for employing the radial tool whereby pressure is applied via the tailstock*

15.15 *Knurled work (left) and the completed tool (right)*

OPERATION

The work is prepared by facing, then relieving the central area to give an outer ring having a radial width of perhaps 5mm. The tool is then mounted in the toolpost, aiming to have the bar at 90 degrees to the bed and the wheel set up at center height and positioned to engage with the ring. Using a low speed and adding oil, the saddle is moved to feed the wheel along to just contact the work. Pressure can then be applied using the tailstock. **Photo 15.14** shows the result of the first trial on a piece of scrap bar.

No provision has been made to retain the wheel on the pin. In use, the applied forces keep it in place, so it just requires care not to lose it in storage and when setting up/taking down. The assembled tool and resultant work are illustrated in **Photo 15.15**.

INDEX

Books for Home Machinists

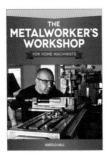
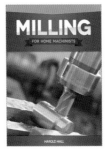
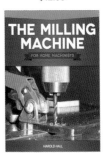

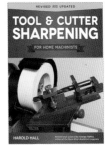